BEYOND EMPOWERMENT

DOUG KIRKPATRICK is a principal of Redshift³, delivering executive coaching, training and business consulting services. He lives in Northern California with his wife, Beth, where he also works and blogs with the Morning Star Self-Management Institute.

BEYOND EMPOWERMENT:

The Age of the Self-Managed Organization

Doug Kirkpatrick

ISBN: 0615470149
ISBN-13: 9780615470146

For Dad

Acknowledgements

❧

This book reflects the wisdom and insight of several very important people. First and foremost, I want to thank Chris J. Rufer, *entrepreneur extraordinaire* and founder of The Morning Star Company, for teaching me through word and example virtually everything I know about business and organizations. His passionate and tireless articulation of bedrock Principles over the last twenty-plus years inspired and informed this book. It would not exist without him.

Paul Green, Jr., my friend and colleague at the Morning Star Self-Management Institute, reviewed the manuscript and provided thoughtful and constructive suggestions for improvement. His assistance was, as always, invaluable.

Thanks go to the people who freely gave of their valuable time to teach the secrets of their respective organizations: Joyce Bowlsbey of W.L. Gore and Associates, Inc., Jim Coblin of Nucor, and Carol Kizziah of Delancey Street Foundation. I am grateful to all of them for generously sharing their experiences.

Roger Burlton of the Process Renewal Group is a vigorous advocate of superior business process management, and helped me appreciate the nexus between process excellence and effective self-management. Dennis Rohan, my personal executive coach and mentor of almost thirty years, instilled in me a deep appreciation for the value of coaching. Their influence on this book was significant.

My two editors, Mike Valentino and Heather Kirkpatrick, are superb wordsmiths who made all the difference.

Finally, I wish to thank my friends and colleagues at The Morning Star Company (and its affiliates), past and present, for manifesting self-management each and every day at work. They are true pioneers.

Contents

∾

Chapter One: Reflections

Todd Brookstone squinted hard into the springtime sun and took a long drink from his canteen. He had come to this side hill overlooking the Santiam River for a weekend of mountain biking and thoughtful introspection. The thirty-two-year-old entrepreneur had a lot on his mind as he contemplated future strategy for his business, even as he reflected on the mostly successful ups and downs of the last four years.

As he sat beside his mountain bike and idly contemplated which of two paths to take at the fork of the trail he was on, he remembered with pride the successful startup that he had shepherded into existence four years earlier.

Back in mid-2003, armed with little more than enthusiasm coupled with a detailed business plan and some impressive financial models, Todd had convinced a group of partners to invest in his upstart Willamette Valley food company, BerryWay. Years of observation and study after college had convinced him that new technology, new configurations of plant and equipment, and innovative products and packages could enable him to carve a successful niche in the processed foods market. And so, at the age of 28, he was ready to achieve his entrepreneurial dreams.

After lining up his new partners, he set to work to identify and engage marketing and distribution partners, to find suppliers for fresh berries, create a sales organization, and hire operations personnel. They would need to assemble the equipment, establish quality control systems, and set up administrative and financial processes. Though extraordinarily challenging, Todd found the work invigorating and enthusing. He thrived on the daily challenges and opportunities. Eighty-hour weeks became the norm as he strove to bring his new factory into operation.

Todd's mentor, Sean Baker, had guided the young entrepreneur through most of the start-up phase. The president of one of the equipment suppliers that Todd brought in as a partner, Sean had seen Todd's promise immediately and appreciated the sophistication of his financial models. There were no obvious business scenarios that Todd had not already modeled in order to play "what-if" games–with potential outcomes both good and bad. Todd had obviously factored all conceivable risk factors into his thinking. The models, and Todd's winning personality, had convinced Sean to invest in the new venture. Sean also appreciated Todd's serious sense of stewardship, which give him a comfort level that Todd would manage his fifty million dollar investment from Sean with a high degree of care.

Sean had also brought Todd into contact with the bankers needed to finance the operation, particularly Steve Cameron, who handled commercial for the local branch of his national bank. Steve had been a banker for some twenty-five years and had seen his share of business proposals, good and bad. Upon their first meeting, Steve was immediately impressed with the young man and his energetic salesmanship of ideas. With the help of Sean's ongoing mentoring, Todd convinced Steve to become the lead bank on his project, offering construction loans and a line of credit totaling almost $100 million.

After the partners and financing were in place, Todd began to engineer his new factory design, first working at home with his own PC-based CAD program, and then taking his drawings to equipment suppliers for their input. He wisely found other mentors in the engineering and equipment community, who schooled him on the nuances of installing and operating their machines for maximum throughput. Within a few months, he had finished his conceptual designs and was ready to get final civil-engineered blueprints, piping and instrumentation diagrams, and necessary land and permits. Armed with the drawings, Todd found an experienced engineering firm to complete blueprints and a respected construction firm to do the installation.

Following a brief search, one of Todd's friends happened to come across a piece of Willamette Valley land that would be perfect for a new food factory. The site offered utilities, road and rail access, infrastructure in the form of water and sewage facilities, and it was conveniently located in a rural area far from homeowners who might object to having a noisy factory in their backyard. Todd instantly recognized the potential of the location and set about acquiring it. Within a month he completed the purchase and began the permit process. Since the land already had the proper industrial zoning, there was no reason to believe that any glitches would occur on that front.

Todd needed some reliable growers for the fresh ingredients required for his recipes for syrups, jams, jellies and toppings. Fortunately, there were some large, cost-effective fruit and vegetable growers in the area that befriended Todd when they learned about his new factory. They eagerly signed up with Todd for multi-year supply agreements that took some of the guesswork out of their annual strategizing about what to grow, how much and for whom. This freed them up to concentrate every year on doing what they do best–growing–and less on trying to decide what volumes to harvest every season.

It was now early September 2003, and if Todd was going to have the new factory up and running by July of 2004, it would be imperative to have fruit acreage formally contracted by the end of January. The project clock was ticking, inexorably, toward success or failure.

On the sales side, Todd began to work with large marketers of Willamette Valley, Oregon food products, in order to lock in long-term win-win supply agreements. His strategy was simple: create great products, be the low-cost producer, and excel at marketing. He felt that even if the long-term supply contracts weren't as profitable as short-term agreements, so long as his costs were covered he could guarantee a profit to the bank and his partners, and use any excess supply to try and capture additional profits on the open market.

Sandra Albertson, VP of Operations at Synergy Foods, a large distributor, represented one long-term customer. Todd and

Sandra negotiated a long-term agreement that met both Todd's need for a long-term profit, and Sandra's need for long-term supply at a reasonable price. As with his suppliers, Todd was able to learn a great deal from Sandra's deep experience in the food industry to understand the business drivers of marketing Willamette Valley-sourced foods in a global marketplace. Sandra enjoyed mentoring the young entrepreneur, and knew that it would only help her own business if Todd did a great job in his. A nice benefit of Todd's long-term sales agreement was the comfort level it gave his financial backers, especially Steve Cameron.

With his partners, bankers, growers, equipment suppliers, engineers, installers, long-term customers and land in place, and with his permits on the way, Todd was ready to enter the next, most challenging phase of being an entrepreneur: hiring and dealing with employees.

He had no clear concept of how to organize his factory people-wise, other than knowing he needed talent in various areas to accomplish his mission of providing customers with great-tasting fresh berry products at the lowest possible cost. Bills were starting to come in from the engineering firm and the county planning department, and actual construction was imminent. Therefore, it was imperative to have an administrative structure in place to deal with cash flowing into and out of the organization, keep track of permits, and gear up to do the rest of the hiring needed to start up the operation.

One of Todd's friends suggested that he set up an advisory board of trusted mentors to advise him on jugular issues in an informal way. Never one to turn down a good idea, Todd asked his primary mentor, Sean, along with Bill Burke, the designer of Todd's primary berry-making equipment, and Sandra from Synergy, to act as his informal advisory panel. They all agreed enthusiastically, drawn by Todd's engaging personality as well as the chance to be on the inside of the largest manufacturing start-up in the area in at least fifteen years. The community was soon abuzz with rumors about the number of high-paying jobs that would become available when the factory started up. People hoped that Todd's project might help ease the area's high unemployment rate. Todd had no power to stop the rumors, even if he had wanted to, but the hopes of the community did instill in him a sense of purpose and a strong desire to not let them down.

Todd convened his advisory board on a Tuesday morning at Sean's office, and laid out his concerns. "I need a financial controller to take charge of the bills and draw funds from our construction loans, and to handle all the high-level financial tasks, like budgeting and accounting, thereafter," he began. "Then I need a production manager, quality control director, and raw product acquisition manager. I'll be the general manager for the time being. How am I supposed to go about this stuff, having never done it before?"

Sean smiled sympathetically at Todd and said, "I've got a good financial accountant that just finished a project for me and has some spare workload capacity. Why don't you talk to her and see if you think she can handle the workload. If you're OK with her, I'll let you hire her on if she's interested, as long as you start her at the same salary she's at right now."

Sandra and Bill thought that made great sense, given Sean's endorsement. "You could go into recruitment mode and try to hire the best available candidate on the job market," Sandra said, "but your immediate need is to get someone to handle the cash going in and out of your company and get ready for full operations. You don't look like you have time to do a full-blown candidate search right now. And if the person Sean is suggesting is qualified and passes the test with you, and later doesn't work out, I assume Sean can hire her back, since he's already happy with her work. Right, Sean?"

Sean nodded affirmatively.

Bill added, "If you're talking about Deborah Moore, she completed an internship with us when she was in college. You can't ask for a better work ethic combined with personality and intelligence."

Thinking about the stacks of invoices that sat on his desk awaiting payment, and the number of tasks he had lined up for himself the following day, Todd nodded and smiled. "Thanks a lot, you guys. Sean, if you can have Deborah give me a call, I'd like to meet with her as soon as possible. But now I have another problem. I need some additional top talent for production, acquisition, QC, and marketing. Could you guys meet without me and put together a game plan on how to get the talent we're going to need to run this company? If Deborah works out, my immediate problem is solved, but we're going to need even more talent in the near future for this venture to succeed. I've got to run now. Can you three continue this meeting and get back to me by next Wednesday with some suggestions?"

Sean, Sandra and Bill smiled and nodded, appreciating the seriousness of their entrepreneurial friend. Bill piped up, "You'd better get back to work, Todd. There's a factory going up on the edge of town, you know."

Todd left with a goodbye wave and a laugh, turning his thoughts to the other people whose help he would need to be successful.

Two days later, Todd met Deborah at Sean's office and interviewed her, describing in detail his expectations for the financial controller position as well as his immediate, pressing needs. After a thorough, two-hour conversation, Todd was satisfied that Deborah would do a fine job, and she was excited for the opportunity and grateful to be considered. After nailing down the specifics of salary and benefits, Deborah asked: "Can I start on Monday?"

With a grin, Todd declared, "Absolutely! Let me call Sean." Todd asked Sean to come in so he could tell him the good news in person. Sean offered temporary space to his employee and her new boss. With one more task out of the way, Todd began to prepare for the even greater challenges ahead.

A week later, the advisory board sat down with Todd to discuss next steps. Deborah had already taken the stack of construction bills, written checks out of Todd's checkbook, and prepared them for signature. She had also delved into the construction budget, reviewed the bank agreements, met with Steve Cameron to discuss funding procedures, and created a temporary filing system. Todd could not have been happier with the workload she was already taking off his shoulders.

"Well, board, what should I do next?" Todd asked half-jokingly. The board members were well aware that Todd had already given a great deal of thought to the staffing question, but he was eager to hear their words of advice before going any further.

"Here's what we came up with, Todd," Bill started. "It's clear that you need top-notch talent in each of the identified managerial slots. There's no way you can be successful without having the right people in the right jobs at the right time. The right time means, when you start up. So here's what we propose. As advisory board members, we'll take each of the identified managerial positions and create a competency model with you—meaning we need to find out from you what a person in each of these positions needs to know to do their job well. We'll also need to know what kind of specific business results you expect from each manager–that will make it possible for you to appraise their performance later on. We didn't have time to do that in Deborah's case, but she was a proven performer. The next wave of hiring will bring in people we don't know, a riskier proposition. We need to find out from you what a quality control manager needs to know to be successful, and then create a job description and define a salary range and hire to that. Since we can't 'promote from within', since there's no 'within' to promote from yet, we'll have to do a full-court press of tapping our personal networks and recruiting from the outside. We all know some excellent recruiters, so that's no problem. The sooner we get them working on this the quicker we can have the talent in place. You'll need to survey your own personal network as well, Todd—even though you're busy these days. And you'll have to update your budgets to reflect possible recruiting costs, generally twenty-five percent of the first year's salary. Are you good with that game plan?"

"Do I have a choice?" Todd replied with a pained grin, mentally adding the hours required to his already impossible schedule.

"We'll split the major jobs up between us and meet with you when it's convenient to create the competency models, job descriptions and results expectations for each of these key jobs," Sandra added. "I'll take the QC Manager and the Raw Product Acquisition Manager," she continued. "The sooner we get started the sooner we can have people in place—when do you want to meet?"

"How about first thing tomorrow morning?"

Sandra nodded her acceptance. "I think it will take a couple of hours of interviewing for each job, just to get the basics nailed down. I can clean up the verbiage and wordsmith a job description later on, to save you time. Bill will sit with you and discuss the production manager, which may take longer since it's a bigger job. And Sean will meet with you to nail down the marketing manager position. I assume you guys can get together offline on your own. We'll meet again once we have all the key positions defined and before we start formally recruiting, just to check each other's work and make sure everything looks good. Sound good?"

Todd smiled with appreciation for all that his friends and mentors were willing to do for him, knowing his time and financial pressures. "Sounds perfect," he replied. "But I think there's one more position that we should consider. I'm going to need a logistics manager, someone to make sure that we account for every asset and inventory item that moves into or out of the facility, and that can make sure inventory is stored and shipped with perfection. Can one of you help with that one?"

Sean stood up, shook Todd's hand, and declared, "You've got it. I'll take care of that one with you."

Todd thanked all of his board members, shook hands, and left, feeling a lot better about his project than before the meeting. It was one thing to prepare engineered drawings, hire contractors, read bank agreements, and even negotiate with the county over roads and permits, and quite another to deal with employees. The whole project suddenly seemed larger than ever.

Two weeks later, the individual position meetings concluded and Todd met once again with his advisory board. "Well, that was a lot of work," Todd noted, "but well worth the effort, I'd say. I feel much better about the kind of people I need to hire to be a part of the management team."

"Great!" Sean spoke up first. "Now let's share this work around and discuss these jobs one by one to see if we've left out anything glaring."

The team spent the next couple of hours going the management jobs one at a time, asking questions about competencies and expectations. Finally, they finished the final job, and Bill said, "I mentioned the project to a couple of people at a Chamber of Commerce meeting the other day, and one of my fellow members said he knew someone that would get a résumé to me for the QC position. I told him that would be great. So the word is already out on the street. But we still have to systematize the recruiting process."

Sandra said, "The three of us have gotten together and created a list of our favorite recruiters. We think there is enough work for more than one recruiter. So we're going to split the jobs up between three recruiters, with each of us managing one recruiter. We'll coordinate with you on interviewing and hiring candidates, since you'll have the ultimate decision authority. Does that work for you, Todd?"

"I couldn't be happier with that approach," he replied, "and for all you guys have done for me. Don't know how I could ever repay you."

Sean noted with a big smile, "Just build a successful factory and make us all look like winners!" Todd grinned at his friends in appreciation, shook hands, and went back to the job site for a day of observing construction.

This was the competency model, job description and business results expectations the advisory board derived for the job of Marketing Manager:

COMPETENCY MODEL: MARKETING MANAGER
Overall Competencies:
Emotional Intelligence (with respect to all stakeholders)
Communication skills (leadership, teamwork, customer relationships)
Technical skills (CRM systems skills, spreadsheet skills, business analytics)
Organizational skills (personal, collegial, leadership)
Adaptation skills (changes in the culture or organizational ecosystem)
Marketing-Specific Competencies:
Design and develop sales and marketing strategies for products
Define market segments
Define market territories and regions
Define product mix based on supply and demand forecasts
Define sales targets, profit targets and sales volumes
Develop new customers
Assist in the design of new products and product extensions
Launch new products when developed
Implement market survey and focus group data collection
Maintain and manage sales and marketing budgets
Implement electronic marketing and promotional discount campaigns
Define focused communication strategies
Implement client databases and CRM systems
Define advertising strategy and implement approved advertising campaigns
Define and implement public relations strategies
Define and implement sales strategy
Effectively manage key accounts

Effectively lead the sales and marketing team and activities
Effectively monitor sales and marketing team performance, and provide relevant feedback
Effectively interface with production to meet customer requirements
Effectively interface with distribution and logistics to insure order fulfillment
Technical Competencies:
Technical product knowledge
Market sector knowledge
Negotiating skills
Market research skills
CRM package knowledge
Spreadsheet skills
Marketing strategic planning skills
Organizational and leadership skills
Ability to develop brand awareness
Ability to handle customer questions and complaints effectively
Mathematical ability; high-level computation skills; pricing analysis skills
Quality assurance and quality control skills
Knowledge of multiple business analysis techniques (i.e. Pareto analysis)
Budget management skills
Sales and marketing legal knowledge
Knowledge and familiarity of INCOTerms for export
Knowledge of product recall processes
Business Process Management (BPM) skills
Knowledge of sales and marketing ethics

JOB DESCRIPTION: MARKETING MANAGER

Company and Position

BerryWay needs a Marketing Manager who will report directly to the CEO/ owner. This position is a tremendous opportunity to get in on the ground floor with an exciting startup Willamette Valley food company.

Our mission is to produce Willamette Valley-sourced food products that delight customers throughout North America and the world.

The candidate should be have an entrepreneurial mindset and be passionate about Willamette Valley foods. They must have a strong background in sales, marketing and distribution with at least five (5) years of sales and marketing experience leading demonstrably high-performance teams.

The candidate must be innovative in acquiring customers, possess the highest standards of honesty and integrity, and execute sales and marketing plans with alacrity and with measurable results.

The successful candidate will:

Sell Product

- *Profitably grow BerryWay product sales and achieve all volume targets*

- *Brand the name BerryWay in the minds of all prospective buyers in North America*

- *Provide oversight for all negotiations regarding pricing and contract terms and conditions*

- *Acquire all necessary resources, including developing relationships and engaging partners, to fulfill sales plans*

Drive Teamwork

- *Organize and motivate a sales and marketing team with the capability of selling into both the foodservice and retail markets*

- *Objectively measure and report performance results against targets*

- *Manage the activities of sales team members and provide necessary feedback*

Plan

- *Forecast sales volumes and profit margins*

- *Plan and implement a profitable product mix*

- *Achieve mutually agreed revenue and profit targets*

- *Oversee marketing expense budgets*

- *Work with production, raw product acquisition and quality control to meet the needs of customers and maximize the efficient use of resources*

Innovate

- *Design and execute approved advertising campaigns*

- *Design complex financial models that facilitate accurate resource management*

- *Assist Research & Development in developing new products and services*

Possess the Following Qualifications

- *Bachelor's Degree or Masters Degree in Business*

- *Strong negotiation, communication and spreadsheet skills*

- *Passion for food, especially Willamette Valley-sourced food*

- *At least five years experience effectively leading sales teams*

- *Willingness to travel extensively*

Our Process
Interested parties should contact Mr. Ron Golden at Process Recruiters, Inc., rgolden@processrecruiters.com. Please include résumé. The CEO/owner and his team of advisors will conduct all interviews.

Compensation
Compensation is commensurate with ability and experience level. A competitive and attractive salary and benefits package will accompany this position.

EXPECTATIONS FOR BUSINESS RESULTS: MARKETING MANAGER
• *Achieve $40 million in annual sales within two years*
• *Maintain average profit margins of at least 2.5%*
• *Receive fewer than five customer complaints per million cases*
• *Contract with at least one new major distributor per month*
• *Launch at least one new product per year (at least $1mm sales)*
• *Maintain at least a 90% customer satisfaction rating*

Meanwhile, the clock was ticking on Todd's new factory. He had to contract with growers for their crops in the winter, after Christmas, but before spring in order to insure availability of fresh produce for the summer production season. It was now mid-March, and the factory was still only one-third complete, although with more than one hundred contractors on site the work was progressing quickly. Growers with committed acreage were starting to get nervous, knowing that their contracts with Todd would not be worth much without an operating factory.

Todd had begun interviewing managerial candidates for the various positions, and had hired a Quality Control Manager, Maria Padilla; Raw Product Acquisition Manager, Kyle Johnson; Marketing Manager, Mike Towers; Financial Controller,

Deborah, who continued to do a great job, and a Distribution Manager, Cathy Sampson. He was still working on hiring a Production Manager, and had a few candidates, but couldn't get excited about any of them. He decided that he could hold off on that position for a while in order to get the right person for the job.

Todd developed a deep appreciation for the model that his advisory board had introduced to him; namely, identifying competencies, creating a solid job description, and defining business results expectations. He decided that he would cascade that model down to each of his new managers, after working with them to determine the number and types of jobs required in each area. His Marketing Manager, Mike Towers, enthusiastically embraced the methodology and worked out the need for five initial salespeople and a sales assistant, and created the competency model, job description and expectations in record time. Todd provided the names of some recruiters, and tasked Mike with going out to the labor market and acquiring the needed talent. Todd made sure to include "talent acquisition" in Mike's job description, and "acquiring needed talent" in Mike's business results expectations. While Todd retained the right to interview and make the final hiring decisions on the permanent marketing team, he was confident in Mike's motivation to find the best people available.

The young entrepreneur realized that he would have to acquire a cadre of talented technicians as soon as possible, with or without a production manager on board. For a factory designed to be capital-intensive and driven by large pieces of machinery and technology, it would be too risky not to have the technicians who would operate the equipment also be involved with the installation, to get a jump up the learning curve and make improvements prior to commissioning.

One night after a hot, dusty day on the construction site, Todd pulled out his factory layout diagrams and began to theorize how many technicians would be necessary. There were six major systems in the factory, each containing between five and ten million dollars of equipment. It made sense to Todd to have at least one technical leader dedicated to each system. Since the factory was designed for 24/7 operations during the production season, Todd was going to have to insist on cross training between areas so that technicians from any area could be responsible for operations during any shift at any time of the day or night. That meant that by his calculus he would need six technicians, each with a high level of skill in their own areas of expertise as well as working knowledge of the other areas and the capacity to pick up what they didn't already know. He needed technicians for fresh fruit receiving, washing and processing, packaging, electrical and automation, steam generation, and utility systems. He pulled up his word processing template to begin creating a competency model for the packaging operation, and promptly fell asleep at his desk. Tomorrow would be another day.

The following morning, Todd and Deborah met with Steve Cameron to review the loan covenants, followed by a meeting between Todd and his growers regarding their nervousness about the pace of construction. Todd spent about two hours mollifying them, then headed back to his home office. A couple of voicemails awaited him, one about a delay in delivering some critical canning equipment, and the other about a problem with his course-of-construction insurance policy. There wasn't anything to be done about the delayed equipment; as long as it was up and running by the first of July he would be happy, although any delays were worrisome. He decided to expand Deborah's job description to handle insurance matters, it was well within her bandwidth and he had more critical things to attend to at the moment.

Todd allowed himself a brief respite to close his eyes at his desk and let his mind drift for a moment. At this particular point in the project, he had many more tasks to do than he had time to do them. In a flash, a key insight came to him that he would thank himself for later: he needed help in the human resources arena; and the sooner the better. He would need to maintain the ultimate decision authority over the hiring of key personnel, but a good HR hand could leverage his time writing up competencies, job descriptions, and expectations; not to mention lining up interviews and filtering résumés. As Todd flashed on the hundred-plus seasonal employees that would be required in the next two months, the need for a superb human resources manager became even more evident. There was no way Todd could handle the human resources task himself. It was time to call another meeting of the advisory board.

Sean, Sandra, Bill and Todd met two days later at Sean's office. Todd laid out the requirement for HR talent as he saw it. After a few minutes of discussion, Sandra noted that her company had just done a candidate search for a new head of human resources, and narrowed it down to two excellent candidates. She would check with the candidate not chosen about availability; if still available and interested, she would forward the résumé to Todd. She offered to work with Todd immediately after the board meeting to rapidly create a competency model, job description, and set of expectations that would work. Todd, hugely grateful as always, accepted her offer.

Three days later, armed with the excellent job description that Sandra had helped him create, Todd interviewed Teresa Williams for the job of Human Resources Manager. He found her to meet all the identified competencies, and to project a warm, friendly personality (a plus, Todd thought, in a position dealing with human beings). Teresa had no objections to any of the business results expectations. When the interview concluded, she asked, "There's a ton of work to do. When can I start?" Todd replied, "Tomorrow, if you like." The next day, Teresa began the significant work of finishing the competencies, descriptions and expectations for the six technical leaders, as well as the eight jobs represented by the one hundred seasonal workers. That was a lot of talent to acquire in a short period of time. She had no time to lose.

As the end of April approached, Teresa had proven herself worthy. She had fully defined the six technical jobs with Todd's input, and had initiated search and interview processes that resulted in four of the six leaders being on board, with multiple candidates for the two remaining key positions. She had created a matrix for seasonal workforce requirements, identifying the jobs that would be hardest to fill and designing a strategy for each of them, while establishing a process for advertising, collecting résumés, and prioritizing the huge flow of résumés that were arriving daily.

Now that she had most of the technical leaders on board, she was able to involve them in the process of making the final decisions for their respective areas. Todd had, uncharacteristically, stepped back from the process of hiring seasonal employees. He had too much on his plate already to be involved in hiring every last employee. He was deeply involved in hiring the technicians, however, and proved to be extraordinarily selective about who filled those slots. He knew that the technical leaders would be the primary source of information and feedback for the seasonal workforce, and the wrong person in a technical position would invite problems, and perhaps even draw the attention of a union. He was determined that all people would be treated fairly and straightforwardly, and he could not tolerate any imperious behavior that reflected poorly on his company. Everyone at BerryWay was entitled to a full measure of dignity at work.

Todd had everything in place and could at last feel comfortable with the progress being made to staff the new factory. He was always comfortable with the progress of construction: equipment arrived on schedule, with a few exceptions, construction workers showed up for work, bills got paid, buildings went up. Now he could breathe just a little bit easier that the factory would be properly staffed for its first year, with one notable exception: his production manager, the most important spoke in the operations wheel.

It was now mid-May, with production slated to start in just over six weeks. Todd needed a production manager onboard as soon as possible to give the person a chance to understand the operation prior to startup. He was fully cognizant that if the position went unfilled, he would be stressed to the breaking point by the sheer volume of rapid-fire operational decisions. He needed someone with focus, drive and the ability to see the big picture, and he needed that person sooner rather than later.

The following day, he convened an emergency meeting of his advisory board, and laid out his concern over the inability to find a production manager. After a long silence, Sean spoke up, saying, "This one may require some out-of-the-box thinking. We've been working with a small set of recruiters up to now, plus some trade magazine advertising. Obviously, this process hasn't yielded the right candidate. I belong to an executive group that has some representatives of large, national recruiting companies. Since we already have a superb job description, I can pull on my contacts and escalate this to a national search. We may have to swallow some relocation costs, but it sounds like it will be worthwhile to get the right person. I'll get on it this afternoon." The other group members nodded in agreement and appreciation at Sean's initiative. With that major headache firmly delegated to his trusted mentor, Todd thanked the group and confidently headed back to the jobsite.

Three weeks later, Todd had his production manager. Scott Thorsen, a seasoned industry veteran from the other side of the country, had been quietly looking for an opportunity since his company had begun downsizing. When he heard about Todd's startup, he jumped on the next plane to the West Coast for an interview. Todd was impressed with his business acumen, technical ability, and breadth of experience. Scott was, seemingly, the ideal candidate for the job. After some fast negotiations over salary and benefits, Scott was on board and at the jobsite, with three weeks to spare before startup. The team was, at last, complete.

On June 30th the first loads of berries rolled into the factory for weighing, grading and washing, and further processing according to Todd's proprietary recipes into the kind of products that he was confident would make a big splash in the market. Todd watched apprehensively as the loads entered the processing equipment, proud of the employees that were doing such a careful job as well as of his advisory board that had come through for him when he needed them most. He worked for a solid twenty-four hours the first day watching every aspect of the operation, culminating in the first jars of labeled berry toppings coming off the production lines to be palletized, shrink-wrapped and stored for shipment to Sandra's factory thirty miles away. He went home and slept better than he had in a long time.

Chapter Two: Challenges

໑ລ

Todd took another long drink from his canteen, wiped his forehead with a bandana, and continued to reflect on the lessons of the past four years. BerryWay had gone on to take a ten percent share of the fruit condiment market thanks to his superb cost structure, which gave him greater pricing flexibility than most of his competitors, and also due to the excellence of his sales and marketing team, who seemed to be hitting on all cylinders. His clearly articulated business strategy was unfolding better than he could have hoped. Mike and his sales and marketing staff were proving to be top-notch. It also hadn't hurt to have a new, state-of-the-art research and development lab, under the direction of his Quality Control manager, Maria, to create innovative and profitable products on a regular basis. Mike and Maria worked well together in positioning products for specific customers and their particular needs. Both were willing to hop on a plane at a moment's notice to visit any distributor that had a technical question or concern about their product. Todd was grateful to have such a proactive pair of managers to interface with his customers.

The only year of four that wasn't profitable was Year One, primarily due to a raw product cost squeeze, coupled with some extra seasonal employees that proved unnecessary. Todd quickly learned that the fixed cost portion of his payroll was significant, and that some overtime could be a lot cheaper than having extra people on the payroll who weren't as productive as they could have been.

He also came to appreciate his financial controller, Deborah, who set up financial systems designed to find every possible discount available from suppliers and collect every dollar owed by customers in a timely fashion. She had shown real initiative in taking over the risk management function too, and was collaborating well with Teresa on designing competitive benefits packages for Todd's approval. They had just finished implementing a company-match 401k that became a huge hit with employees (partly due to the plan's robust investment options), and were looking forward to measuring retention rates and conducting employee surveys to support the wisdom of their decision. Todd was also pleased that Deborah had taken over the bulk of his banking relationship with Steve Cameron, who was impressed with the quality of the financial statements and the consistency with which BerryWay was meeting or exceeding its loan covenants. Steve was able to brag about his account with his higher-ups at the bank, who were kiddingly jealous of his success in approving what many thought to be a risky loan four years earlier.

Teresa turned out to be a better human resources manager than Todd expected, having hired and on-boarded nearly one hundred seasonal employees that first year, with a ninety percent return rate from year to year. She was popular with the workforce, and always took time to answer questions and listen to employee concerns. Her friendly manner coupled with a solid background in human resources management gave Todd a great deal of confidence Teresa and her staff.

Still, things could be better. Scott, while technically competent, didn't like to make decisions quickly, especially when it came to people. When one of his six production supervisors engaged in sexual harassment on the job, Scott failed to swiftly address the behavior. When the evidence against the supervisor became irrefutable, BerryWay had to endure a state labor board investigation, which confirmed the inexcusable reporting delay. The company paid a significant fine, and Scott was forced to fire the supervisor. Scott's failure to confront issues in the workplace, and passive approach to harmful conflict, was proving costly. The conflicts in Scott's team were eating away at morale like a slow acid bath.

Furthermore, Todd's open door policy resulted in many employees coming to him directly with issues and problems that Scott should have been able to easily handle. Things were reaching a point where Scott's inability to deal with people issues was starting to overwhelm his ability to resolve technical production concerns and drive production. Todd engaged Scott in several conversations about his concerns, but things never seemed to improve. Todd himself had to let another of the six production supervisors go, for fundamental performance reasons—something Scott should have seen and dealt with long before. The production supervisors and Scott were at the very heart of production, where the product was created for customers. Further lack of solid performance was inconceivable to Todd. Something would have to be done regarding Scott, and soon.

Todd's other source of concern involved his Raw Product Acquisition manager, Kyle. For months, Todd had been requesting a quantitative analysis of all growers within a two hundred mile radius, so that relationships could be cultivated to secure future supplies of high-quality raw product. Kyle apparently found it more interesting to pursue new technology initiatives, which appealed to his scientific background. While some of Kyle's new initiatives proved moderately helpful, they weren't doing much to boost the strategy of the company in developing new sources of supply. Although Todd knew and appreciated Kyle's strengths, and they had been receiving adequate quantities of product every year, the quality of the berries and fruits had started to slip. In addition, growers were sometimes not delivering the promised degrees of ripeness, which were critical to the product recipes that Todd's customers counted on—forcing him to renegotiate quality specifications with customers or borrow varieties from one customer in order to satisfy another. Being forced to compensate for Kyle's mistakes and watching the grower strategy stagnate was not Todd's idea of good execution. He gradually became aware that he would have to address Kyle's situation sooner rather than later.

Complicating his calculus, Todd was developing an entrepreneurial strategy to create an entirely new company, one with a fuller line of products, including juices, flavorings, and candies. He planned to offer the opportunity to his partners, and offer expanded responsibilities to his managerial staff. Unless he confronted the concerns he had with Scott and Kyle, however, it would be imprudent to talk with them about increasing their career opportunities in a new venture. So far he had been getting by with back of the envelope performance appraisals, done once a year before Christmas. He realized that he hadn't done an especially good job of conducting those conversations— Teresa had done a better job performing appraisals for the seasonal workforce. One way or the other, he needed to soon have some very difficult conversations.

"Why," Todd often wondered to himself, "can't people in the workplace hold each other accountable for performance?" He realized that he was as guilty as anyone in that regard. After all, without workplace performance, there are no satisfied customers. He realized that the two most acute areas of leadership concern in his factory, production and acquisition, were also the most highly structured. When he started the factory, he hadn't given much thought to the notion of organizational structure, adopting the same structure as the traditionally hierarchical, unionized plant fifty miles away. At the time, Todd thought that must be the way to go: bring in managers, put staff under the managers, and let the managers manage the staff. Have a hierarchy of bosses, and let the subordinates answer to the bosses for their day-to-day performance. Have the bosses appraise performance and hand out any bonuses or pats on the back, as well as discipline. Keep the wage scale competitive. Direction and strategy will come from the top (Todd), and be communicated to the managers who should be smart enough to absorb it. Then they can chunk the information down to their subordinates in bite-sized pieces until everyone is rowing in the same direction. It seemed to make sense at the time...but did it really?

Todd thought about his happy home life. He had gotten married the previous year, and his wife Sarah was expecting a baby in a few months. He thought to himself: "Why can't people in the workplace treat each other like a family? After all, Sarah and I make all kinds of jugular decisions in our family without one us being the 'boss'. What's the difference between a family and a workplace?"

He had been reading a lot lately about liberating civil principles. It seemed clear that virtually all human interaction could be distilled down to two basic principles, which, if followed, would allow for extraordinarily productive interaction in the workplace as well as in the rest of society.

The principles:

First, people should keep their commitments to others.

Second, people should not use force against others or their property.

Todd thought back on all the incidents where people had come to him to appeal a firing by one of the production supervisors. In almost every case, further investigation showed a lack of substantiation by the supervisor, or sloppy documentation of probable lack of performance. Todd had reversed all of these decisions except one, where the supervisor had actually done a good job of documenting and trying to turn around the employee. But Todd's frustration with the system was becoming palpable, and starting to drain him. The problems were too time-consuming, the psychic energy lost too stressful. There had to be a better way. Could he adapt the foundational principles of a harmonious and prosperous civil society to the workplace?

Likewise, Todd reflected on the second principle of civil society: people should keep their commitments to others. He had talked to Kyle on more than one occasion about the need for a quantitative supply analysis. Somehow, Kyle always had an excuse, despite making a specific commitment to the new strategy. Todd reflected on the discrepancy between words and actions, and recognized the full extent of the opportunity cost of Kyle not keeping his explicit commitments. Todd was beginning to lose confidence in the traditional organizational structure he had adopted. There had to be a better way.

Todd stood up with his bike, savored one last look at the fast-flowing water of the Santiam River, and gazed down at the fork in the trail. The right fork was obscured with brushwood from the previous winter; the left fork was well worn and clear. Ignoring the obstructions, he took the right fork. His mind was full of ideas and he wanted to get to work.

Chapter Three: A New Beginning

∾

As he navigated his bike down the rough path, Todd became convinced that his original organization structure was more hindrance than help. It wasn't driving accountability, it wasn't leveraging his time, and it wasn't working in two critical areas of the operation. He suspected that matters could be even worse than he imagined, if people were papering over their differences and failing to hold each other accountable on the factory floor, especially in production operations. It was time to blow up the old structure, grab a clean sheet of paper and a pencil, and start over with his two key principles. Some employees would not be happy with the results, but there would be a principled structure that delivered results. Todd would make sure of that.

The next morning, he spread out some paper on his large maple desk at his Santiam River vacation cabin, and started to draft a new organizational charter based on his two basic civil principles. As he pondered the large, flat work surface of his desk, it occurred to him that the ideal organization structure should be flat. It became increasingly clear to him that many of the people problems he had experienced resulted from managers or supervisors thoughtlessly exercising their position, power and authority, which others found intimidating at worst and imperfectly informed at best. While he himself had been forced to fire a few people based on legal imperatives, it seemed to Todd that an organizational structure that put all employees on the same footing with respect to authority was the only structure that made sense.

As he contemplated the ramifications of a totally flat organizational structure, he grabbed a freshly sharpened pencil and began outlining. What would flatness look like? First, a flat structure would require no titles. That meant that conceptually, all employees would be on the same footing with respect to each other, no exceptions. That would be a hard sell for some employees, but necessary.

Second, there would be no command authority. Maybe there were institutions that require the authority to issue commands, like the military, but most people don't live their lives subject to such authority, outside of work. Todd thought hard about which business decisions couldn't be made just as well, if not better, through persuasion and influence rather than being dictated. He resolved that all conceivable decisions in his business could be made and carried out through persuasion—even strategic decisions. If an employee can't be persuaded about a course of action, he or she won't be engaged anyway. What better way to drive execution than actually making sure people are committed to a direction in the first place?

Third, Todd recognized that under decent civil principles, people aren't able to "fire" one another. Marriage partners may get divorced using established processes, but people in a marriage are partners, not bosses and subordinates. If he were going to design a truly flat organization, he would have to put everyone on the same footing. No one would have unilateral authority over any other person in his organization, including the authority to fire. Todd could already picture the objections coming from some of his managers over that one. But he would be ready to answer them.

A totally flat organization, as flat as his maple desktop, with no titles and no unilateral command authority, and no one having the authority to fire. Todd was beginning to appreciate the full significance of his ideas. He had been reading the business literature, and had come across several articles about "reducing the number of layers" in various businesses. He thought about having no layers. Zero. He wondered what his business brethren would think about such an outlandish plan. Then he set those thoughts aside and continued his work. He wasn't really interested in what other leaders thought or did. His focus was rightfully on his own company and his own industry, where he was successful and respected. While he appreciated the significance of his thinking, his main concern was making what he owned work even better. So, grabbing a hot cup of coffee, he allowed himself a glance out the window and pushed on.

In a flat organization without titles, Todd reasoned, there would be a need for a term to better reflect the relationship of his employees to the company and to each other. He felt that the term "employee" itself was sterile and carried the implication of subservience rather than professional decision-making. He looked up the dictionary definition of "employee", finding it to mean "a person working for another person or a business firm for pay." Disappointed that he had allowed such a clinical term to take hold in his company, he brainstormed several candidates for a new designation, including "associate", "ally", "partner", "colleague", and "teammate". After staring at the list for a few minutes, he settled on "colleague" as the definitive designation. He made a mental note to meet with Teresa as soon as possible to suggest infusing the new term throughout the handbook and the rest of the organization. He liked the dictionary definition of colleague, "To unite or associate with another or with others", and what it implied about voluntary association in pursuit of the overall mission. From now on, his employees would be colleagues, if he could persuade them.

Todd had been to a recent business conference, and talked to a fellow CEO who had recently hired an executive coach for several of his direct reports, and had embraced coaching for his entire workforce. Remembering the great mentoring that he continued to receive from his advisory board, Todd reflected that coaching and mentoring was the model he wanted to adopt and infuse throughout his organization. He wanted colleagues to be able to provide feedback to each other with a coaching approach, rather than just throwing their weight around and pointing out mistakes. He would explicitly embrace a culture of coaching and mentoring. BerryWay colleagues would help each other's professional growth. Todd smiled as he contemplated the human and financial benefits of a positive coaching and mentoring culture.

Todd recognized that there would be situations that would call for colleagues to hold one another accountable. He further recognized that there would be circumstances where such accountability might demand that someone leave the company. There would have to be a process in place that would allow for objective examination of facts, with checks and balances, so that colleagues could hold each other accountable up to and including the termination of employment. Some legal circumstances would require a circumvention of this process. If someone came to work intoxicated, or waving a loaded weapon, there would be no time for due process, and the legal system would not look kindly at any delay in dealing with such a person. On the other hand, he had become aware of a supervisor threatening to fire subordinate production workers for relatively minor mistakes in operating procedure. He had no tolerance for such unnecessary displays of arrogance and power. If that supervisor hadn't had the title of "supervisor", and hadn't had any authority to fire anyone, his threats would have been laughed at, and the workplace would have been more humane and productive.

When circumstances required a serious discussion of performance, however, there would be a process in place in order to continue to achieve the mission of the company. He wrote the words **Accountability Process** on his outline, and began to sketch out some bullet points to fill it out. The first bullet point was: "Have a direct conversation with the person". One of Todd's biggest headaches involved malicious gossip and people that talked behind each other's backs about performance issues. He would explicitly repudiate that option, at least regarding colleague performance, and require that anyone noticing performance or integrity issues with another colleague would be required to directly discuss the issue with that colleague. Anyone not willing to initiate such a discussion would just have to tolerate the situation. Either put up or shut up. Talking behind the person's back would not be an option. In fact, talking behind the person's back would itself become an express violation of the set of principles Todd was developing.

Todd allowed that such a one-on-one discussion would not necessarily resolve a difference of opinion. The next step he wrote down was: "Third party mediator." He theorized that if a discussion between two colleagues didn't resolve the issue, there would have to be a fresh set of eyes to examine the facts and circumstances, hear from both colleagues, and express their thoughts about the points being made on both sides. The mediator would have to be someone trusted by both colleagues, and would have an obligation to hear both sides and articulate their own thoughts about what they had heard. The mediator, however, would not have any power to resolve the issue. That power still belonged to the two colleagues themselves. But the mediator would be in a superb position to keep the discussion on track, and see that the colleagues stick to the facts and stay away of personalities.

It was quite possible, Todd thought, that even a mediated discussion would not result in a resolution of a difference of opinion between two colleagues. This would be especially true, for example, if one colleague were to ask another colleague to terminate their employment for reasons of performance or integrity. Few colleagues could be expected to voluntarily relinquish their jobs without vigorous dissent. Therefore, Todd thought, there must be a final step in the course of due process. If any difference of opinion could not be resolved by direct discussion or mediation, then it would be necessary to convene a panel of colleagues to hear both sides and stay in the conversation until a resolution were reached. If the panel became deadlocked, then Todd would participate in the deliberations and render a final decision. At some point, all disputes must come to an end. Todd left the determination of the size and composition of the panel to a future date. He felt he was making real progress.

Here is the list that Todd completed that morning at his desk:

Keeping Commitments	No Use of Force
• No Titles	
• No Command Authority	
• No Unilateral Authority to Fire	
• Colleagues	
• Coaching and Mentoring Culture	
• Accountability Process	

Todd took a lunch break with a sandwich and coffee, then sat back down at his desk to review what he had written down. His list contained some fairly radical ideas for a manufacturing company, and he was sure that his fellow CEOs would find it somewhat surprising that anyone would attempt to organize a company that way. The anticipated skepticism, however, only convinced him to press forward. There is no doubt, Todd theorized, that other CEOs are having the same kinds of issues that he had experienced. The only difference is that no one had broken down the hierarchy as much as Todd anticipated doing with BerryWay. And now, as he mulled further refinements to his flat organizational structure, he came up with a capstone idea to help him round out the concept.

Todd leaned back in his chair, thinking. His head was swimming with the implications of the experiment he was about to unleash. Although he had some of the basic concepts written down, he began to second-guess himself and question the rationality of some of those ideas. After all, no one to his knowledge had tried the full measure of what he was about to attempt in a significant multi-million dollar enterprise.

As he contemplated the list, Todd felt that while his design had sharply limited the downside of traditional hierarchical organizations—but had he adequately appreciated the potential upside? After all, if all he wanted was to eliminate power trips, there might be other ways to accomplish that. What were the true benefits of flatness? He remembered a photograph he'd seen recently, taken by satellite, of the Korean peninsula at night. South Korea was brightly lit, vibrant with activity. North Korea was dark, save for a pinpoint of light in the capital of Pyongyang. The difference between the two countries? The degree of freedom. Todd's new organization was going to be based on freedom. No one at BerryWay knew better how to perform a job better than the person doing the job. There were no obvious reasons why people shouldn't be free to perform their jobs to the best of their ability according to their own understanding of the needs of the particular job. There were no obvious reasons why people shouldn't be free to innovate new ways to perform their jobs even better. There were no obvious reasons why people shouldn't be free to negotiate changes in their jobs so long as the needs of the organization were met. Todd had identified the foundation of his organization. It was freedom. Freedom to act responsibly in pursuit of the mission. He added it to his list.

He needed a rubric—what was he going to call this type of organization? After a half hour of thinking, eyes closed, he decided that no term better described what he was considering than **self-management.** If a colleague in the business didn't have other-management, meaning a boss, then by default the only source of managerial direction would have to come from one's self and the colleagues who would hold each other accountable through dialogue and persuasion—but not force. Todd was satisfied that he had his rubric. All that remained was to fill in the details. Something inside him told Todd that the easy part was over. He wrote the term **Self-Management** on his list, put down his pencil, and went for a walk.

When he got back, he decided to test out some of his new concepts on Sarah. While she was slicing some peppers for a dinner salad, he asked her, "Honey, how would it be if I became your boss in this family, since, after all, I'm the man and chief breadwinner?"

He said it with such a broad grin that she could not miss the fact that he was kidding, and played along. "And why in the world would I agree to such a ridiculous arrangement?" she rejoined. "I don't see you getting pregnant. And after our baby is born, I can scarcely see you changing any diapers, either!"

"But honey," Todd said, "how will we organize ourselves? How will we decide who does what? How will we manage a budget? Who will pay the bills? Take out the garbage? How does any family manage without a boss?"

Sarah gave him a long, slightly annoyed look. "I guess we'll have to find out," she said. "Maybe we can just agree to divide up the household work based on who does something the best. I'm guessing that I'll be the best at nursing our new baby. Make sense?" she declared with a note of amused finality.

With that, Todd accepted the end of the conversation, and noted to himself that he could now think of no inherent reason why self-management could not apply to the workplace. If human beings were smart and sophisticated enough to get married, have children, take on mortgages, look for jobs, buy cars, go on vacations, save for college, serve in community organizations, and face all the other myriad challenges presented by everyday life, there was no reason that human beings couldn't manage themselves in the workplace. Todd thought, *How in the world did American pioneers settle the West without self-managing? In fact, how did the supervisors in the plant come together in a fantasy football league every year, memorize scores of statistics and follow the intricacies of the NFL free agent market, without self-managing?* His course set, he found himself looking forward to work on Monday morning.

After dinner, Todd and Sarah sat silently holding hands on a couch in front of their big picture window, watching the sun set in the west. When darkness fell, Todd went back to his desk and wrote his rubric at the top of his list, and went to bed.

Self-Management	
Keeping Commitments	No Use of Force
• No Titles	
• No Command Authority	
• No Unilateral Authority to Fire	
• Colleagues	
• Coaching and Mentoring Culture	
• Accountability Process	
• Freedom	

For the next few weeks, Todd read voraciously, trying to absorb any bits of information regarding what he considered a key insight into how to organize a large commercial enterprise. He devoured books and articles about entrepreneurial companies' organizational styles, military command structures (which, he learned to his surprise, can oscillate between command-and-control and pure self-management), and high-tech business performance initiatives. Nothing he read disabused him of his determination to create the world's first large-scale, totally self-managed commercial enterprise. In fact, the more he read, the more he came to believe in self-management. It was time to share some of his thinking with colleagues, and to gauge their reactions. After all, it wouldn't be fair to simply declare that henceforth BerryWay would be a flat, self-managed company. People had joined the company with certain assumptions, and had taken on jobs with titles and expectations. He would have to build support for his ideas one colleague at a time. It was time for a company meeting.

The following Monday at 8:00 a.m. sharp, Todd's managers and supervisors gathered in the spacious cafeteria. The office phones were being handled by an answering service; it was important to Todd that all hands were on deck and distractions kept to a minimum. The low hum of vending machine motors blended with the buzz of conversation when Todd entered the room. Everyone looked up at him with anticipation and curiosity. His meeting memo had stated the topic would be "Organizational Development." No one seemed to quite know what that meant or what to expect from the meeting.

Todd began simply: "I've been doing a lot of thinking and reading lately, as you may have noticed," he started out. "And I've come to some very unique conclusions about how to organize the business. If we debate, discuss, and ultimately agree with my conclusions and adopt my unique ideas, then we'll have something very special. If we debate and discuss and ultimately leave things the way they are, then we'll still have the great company we have today. But I want to start a dialogue with this meeting, and follow up with more meetings, small group discussions, or whatever other formats make sense, because I want to have these ideas fully discussed before we even think about the possibility of adopting any of them. With me so far?"

The colleagues in the room nodded affirmatively. Deborah spoke up first. "Why don't you share some specifics," she suggested. "You've been sharing tidbits with me for the last month. Go ahead and outline your thoughts and give us something to chew on."

Todd nodded in appreciation for her suggestion, and walked to the large white board he had set up earlier, grabbing a marker. At the top of the white board, he wrote **Self-Management**. "This is what I'd like to have a dialogue with you about," he began. "This concept has been burning in my mind for weeks now, and I need to fully vet and discuss it with you. If I'm thinking about using self-management as an organizing principle for the business, and all of you are stakeholders, it's imperative that you participate in this discussion and be engaged." He paused for effect. "Here's why I'm interested in this idea."

"There are two basic principles of human interaction that lead to abundance, happiness and prosperity. One is that no person should use force against another. Second, people should keep their commitments. The first principle underlies most criminal law. The second principle underlies most civil law. Does anyone disagree with the notion that if everyone followed these two simple principles that our world would be a better place to live in?" Todd waited for his words to sink in. "Has anyone here had someone fail to meet a commitment to you at BerryWay, that caused you to not be able to meet one of your own objectives?" Todd watched as about half the room raised their hands. "What would it have been worth if those people had either come through as agreed or met with you to openly renegotiate the commitment? What difference would that have made?" Todd saw the group nod with understanding at the contrast they were envisioning. While his colleagues mulled the topic of commitment, he wrote the words **Key Principles** under **Self-Management**.

Keeping Commitments

Jody, a sales team member, spoke up. "I don't want to get too personal here, but when I needed some hard inventory numbers to assure my customer that we had their required product, they weren't provided until it was too late—and the customer went to Brand X. My colleague assured me that he'd have the information to me by the end of the week, and then he left on vacation without sending it. It cost the company a lot of money to lose that account. When I told my supervisor, he said not to worry about it, that we'd get the customer back eventually. The problem is that it affects my numbers and my bonus, and it's not right. So if what you're proposing is a better way to organize in order to get things done right, I'm all for it."

"Any other thoughts on commitment?" Todd asked. "Do we have agreement that the second principle of human interaction, that people should keep their commitments, is a sound one in guiding organizational behavior?"

While everyone nodded in agreement, Todd took advantage of the teachable moment to drive the point home even deeper.

"What is another word for keeping commitments?" Todd asked the group.

"Honesty?" one person in the back replied.

"Reliability?" another added.

Todd paused and faced the group squarely in the center of the room. "Your answers are all good," he said. "But I'm thinking of another word that really resonates with me. It's called 'integrity'." The group looked at Todd intently, listening closely.

"Integrity is closely related to honesty," he continued. "Honesty, I would argue, has everything to do with making sure that what you're communicating reflects actual circumstances. For example, if you report sales or production output for a given month, the number accurately reflects what was sold or produced." He paused and spoke slowly. "Integrity is the other side of the coin. Integrity has to do with keeping your commitments. It means making sure that your actions reflect what you have already communicated to others. Meaning, if you say you'll do something, you do it. And if you brand yourself as a person that keeps commitments, you will be considered a person of integrity."

"Well, it's obvious that integrity and honesty are important," Phil, a manager sitting in the front row, volunteered. "That applies to everyone, everywhere, all the time. What makes us so unique that we have to spend time discussing it?" the manager asked as he glanced at his watch. "I've got product to make, and spending time in this meeting discussing stuff that we learned in kindergarten isn't helping the contribution margin." He stopped and waited for Todd's response.

Todd answered, "You're right, Phil. We probably all learned at an early age that it's good to have honesty and integrity. But let's have that show of hands again of people who have been let down by associates who have failed to keep commitments." Most of the group again raised their hands, including some who had been reluctant to do so the first time. "So without putting anyone on the spot about specifics, it seems pretty clear to me that what should be automatic doesn't always work in real life. We seem to have a gap between realizing the virtue of integrity and actually keeping workplace commitments. That's a big part of what this meeting is about today."

Todd continued. "It looks like we're in agreement that keeping commitments is the right thing to do. I'll go one step further and propose that keeping your commitments creates economic value and makes you as an individual and the enterprise you work within more valuable." He really had their attention at this point.

"The value of a commitment depends on the level of trust one has in the fulfillment of the commitment. If an inventory of raw fruit is not available at the time of scheduled production, what happens?" Todd asked.

"We shut down the line!" came the swift and accurate answer from the group.

"So if our raw fruit supply colleagues promise available inventory, and that inventory is not there when needed, there is a cost associated with that commitment failure, right?" Heads nodded up and down. Todd continued. "Since we're all interdependent here, there are consequences to not having fruit inventory available on time. The cost is far beyond the additional expense of sourcing the fruit elsewhere. The cost is the inability to run the factory for the period of time when fruit is lacking, the cost of the workers who are being paid to stand around waiting for fruit to arrive, and I'm sure you can think of some more—like gas and electric utilities being wasted. Think of it this way: if you assume that our regular cost of fruit is $15 per ton, and the cost of replacement fruit is $20 per ton, you might be tempted to think the additional cost is only $5 per ton. But you'd be missing the lost contribution margin of $10,000 per hour for the four hours it would probably take to source replacement product—while the factory stood idle awaiting something to run through it.

"And remember, we're a highly seasonal operation. We can't just run extra hours in the winter to make up for lost time in the summer." Heads nodded. "What I'm getting at is this: the value of a commitment is proportional to the degree one can expect that commitment to be fulfilled. What is a commitment worth from a person that doesn't follow through? Not much. How about a commitment that you can count on 100% of the time, and if there's a problem, you can at least count on the person to renegotiate with you? A lot?" The room began to buzz with side conversations. Todd knew that he had hit a nerve, and pressed his points.

"The positive value of commitment reliability and the negative value of commitment unreliability is not merely proportional to the value of the underlying commitment. It is geometrically proportional. Why? Because we, and the outside world, are so interrelated. Finding replacement product, for example. We can't just expect to walk out on the street and hail a cab towing a trailer of fruit for sale. We have to call our database of fruit suppliers until we find someone with extra for sale, usually at exorbitant spot prices. Then we have to negotiate terms, execute contracts, and arrange logistics and quality control. Compared to the value of having our own raw product available at the right time and in the right quantity and at the right price, the cost of supply failure is astronomical. I hope I'm making my point." The silence in the room told him that he was.

"To put it in personal terms, let's say there are two otherwise identical production managers, each making $100,000 per year, but Manager A is 100% reliable in keeping commitments, and Manager B is only 80% reliable. Manager A insures that Sales always receives the agreed-upon product mix for our customers. Manager B promises to supply Sales with sweet berry jam, which would have made a $25,000 profit, but produces semi-sweet jam instead (on one of his unreliable days) which sells at a $35,000 loss. I would be completely justified adjusting salaries and paying Manager B less than 80% of Manager A's salary at any salary level. That 20% unreliability has already cost us seriously more than $20,000—try $60,000 for one missed commitment.

Unreliability is profoundly costly. Reliability is extraordinarily valuable—it is, in fact, precious. I am absolutely willing to pay a premium for proven reliability, by the way."

Todd continued. "Let's talk about branding for a minute. We have brands that we're very proud of and that our customers value with their dollars. What do they value about our products?" Todd queried.

After a few seconds of silence, Teresa spoke up. "Reliability?" she asked.

"Good point!" Todd continued. "Customers appreciate our brands because they know they can count on us for the same quality in every jar, at a fair price. We are known for having great products in our market niche. We're reliable. Did you know that all of you have an individual brand as well?" Todd asked.

Mike spoke for the group and said, "Yes, it makes sense that as individuals we have a brand, especially after the discussion of integrity. We brand ourselves day in and day out through our words and actions. The customers I deal with care a lot about the BerryWay brand—it means a lot to them. And our personal brand should mean a lot to each of us."

"Why is it important?" Todd queried. "Apart from being the right thing to do, why is it important that you brand yourself as a person of integrity, honesty and reliability?" Todd paused for the response.

"Because it's easier to do business with someone of integrity, who keeps their commitments?" Cathy replied.

"Exactly right!" Todd exclaimed. "The cost of doing business with integrity-and-reliability-branded people is lower, and thus more 'profitable' to transact business with. And guess what else? The more profitable it is to do business with you, the more people want to work with you, and the more opportunities you have—that's how people and companies grow. That's how value increases, commercially and personally."

Todd looked at the room of colleagues, who were completely absorbed in the discussion. As he looked out, he felt deep appreciation for their hard work and dedication to the company, and for the success that he and they had enjoyed to this point.

He loved them and their families and felt a deep sense of responsibility to create systems and structures that expressed his appreciation for their efforts. He gave his colleagues a ten-minute break, then looked at his notes to prepare for the next session.

When the group returned from the break, Todd engaged in some Q&A about the topic of keeping commitments, then segued into the other key principle. "OK. We've talked about how important it is to keep commitments, and I think we've discussed that to the point where we're ready to move on. Is that okay with everyone?" Seeing no disagreement, Todd turned to the white board and drew two arrows emanating from the words **Key Principles**. The first arrow he labeled **Keeping Commitments**. The second he labeled **No Use of Force**.

No Use of Force Against Other Persons or Their Property

"How many people here want to be told what to do by a superior when they come to work every day?" Todd asked, raising one eyebrow. "Anyone?" Seeing no hands raised, he continued. "Commanding others doesn't tend to work in everyday life, does it?" Picking on Cathy in the front row, he pursued his line of inquiry. "Do family members appreciate being told what to do, Cathy?"

Smiling, she shook her head from side to side.

"Granted, sometimes command authority is necessary," Todd continued. "You may have to tell a child not to cross the street in traffic. And men and women in uniform have voluntarily subjected themselves to an environment of command and control. But normally, adults don't appreciate being told what to do if they already have an idea of what they should be doing. And I'm interested in making some serious changes in that regard." The room became very quiet.

"Here's what I'm proposing," Todd continued. "I want to obliterate all hierarchy in this organization, beginning as soon as possible. I know some of you have titles, and were hired with certain responsibilities for managing others. But I have to say that there have been some disappointments in that regard. So I'm proposing a radical change, one that might rock this company to its foundations. Since this change is so large, I'm willing to discuss it, hold meetings on it, and evaluate your concerns for the next three months. I will take your concerns and interests fully into account. And if you don't think this change is for you, I will bend over backwards to help you find a more compatible situation, in a way that doesn't cause you financial loss.

"All I ask in return is that if you express concerns and doubts about the change I'm proposing, that those concerns be as concrete and specific as possible. The changes I'm proposing are concrete, and I've thought about them deeply for a long time. So any arguments against change will have to be persuasive—and you know me well enough to know I appreciate facts and logic." Todd paused, letting his comments reverberate throughout the room. "Any questions before I lay out my ideas?" Seeing no objection to continuing, he began to make his case.

"We seem to have contracted a case of 'title creep'," Todd observed. "I had Teresa give me a list of all the titles we have in the company. For a company of only fifty people, we have some of the most evocative titles I've ever heard. My favorite is 'Assistant to the Associate Manager of Raw Product Acquisition'. Bernie, you get the prize today for Most Creative Title!" Bernard Walker, the owner of the title, smiled with slight twinge of embarrassment. "And Bernie, I think you're doing a good job, by the way," Todd observed. "I'm only selecting your title to make my point."

"We have people with command authority over others, but all major personnel disputes seem to end up on my desk anyway. So what's all this command authority worth?" Todd continued. "My sense is that everyone here already knows what they're supposed to be doing...is that right, as far as you can tell, Bernie?" Todd continued his riff. Bernie nodded in agreement.

"Command authority involves the use or implied use of force," said Todd, making a fist to express his point. "The implication is: if I'm your superior, you need to do what I tell you to do. If not, I have the power to discipline or fire you—for insubordination, if nothing else. And since I have the power to evaluate you as a subordinate, I have some power over your career path and over your compensation. By the way, Teresa, is

the insubordination language still in our employee handbook?"
Teresa nodded yes.

"I have come to the conclusion that the use of force is wrong,"
Todd observed. "Force represents coercion against another person or their property. To tell a person what to do on the job
when you have the power to help or hurt a person's career is,
in effect, coercion. And I've decided that I don't like it. If your
path is superior to that of your colleague, you should be able to
persuade them of the benefit of taking a different path. And if
you can't persuade them, perhaps you need to spend a bit more
time thinking through the benefits of taking your path, and how
to communicate them persuasively. And how do know your path
is superior unless you listen to your colleague's explanation of
why they're doing what they're doing?"

The silence in the room was palpable, finally broken by the
voice of Scott Thorsen, Production Manager.

"I can't understand how things will get done in such an environment," Scott asked. "We have customers that depend on us
getting quality product out at a competitive price. As the Production Manager, I'm responsible for making sure that happens.
Are you saying that I'm supposed to influence and persuade employees to make things happen? That just doesn't compute for
me," Scott concluded, shaking his head.

"I know it sounds radical, Scott," Todd gently affirmed. "But
trust me when I say that I'd really like you to think it through and
then shoot holes in it. It really needs to be right, and if it can be
improved through honest critique and dialogue, I'm all for making it better. I'm not the font of all human wisdom, after all."
Scott tilted his head slightly and nodded in agreement.

"Let's think about how decisions get made," Todd continued.
"Who is the best person to make decisions about how, when,
where, and why work gets done?"

He waited for a long time before Maria spoke up. "Well, the
person doing the work, obviously!" she exclaimed, as if any other
answer would be absurd.

"That's what I think, too," Todd agreed. "And if someone
has a different opinion, I think it should be a topic of discussion,

rather than a dictate to do something else, or to do the same thing differently.

"So here's what I'm proposing. I'd like to flatten this organization totally. No titles. No command authority. No unilateral authority to fire, period, even for me. Zero hierarchy, none, nada, zip, zero." Todd was really passionate now, as he launched into the heart of his proposal. "I see a large performance upside to this concept. Freedom is the only system in the world that really works. I want people working here, who have, after all, pledged at least forty hours a week and some many more, to be free to do their jobs to the very best of their ability and professional know-how.

"To the degree that our people are free to perform to the best of their ability, they are also free to innovate change that improves performance even more. There will be no barriers to communication in the workplace—anyone will be able to discuss anything with anyone else regardless of area or process.

"I also believe that we will benefit from better decisions being made," Todd continued. "One person making a decision, even with experience and a stellar track record, cannot possibly account for all the variables that must be considered in making many strategic and operational decisions that affect the work of others. It is imperative that people talk to each other before decisions get made, if they are affecting or being affected by the actions of another person.

"Remember the situation last summer, when we didn't have enough packaging inventory to handle our additional spot production?" Todd reminded his colleagues. "That was a mini-disaster that could easily have been avoided by simple communication. There is really no reason for such situations to occur. I believe that eliminating unilateral command authority will compel colleagues to communicate about decisions that affect each other—since no one will have any authority to tell another colleague to accept change without discussion. I also believe that this communication will result in better decisions being made, since they will be made with the best available information from all those affected.

"I've also decided that I'm not a fan of the word 'employee'," Todd noted. "The word 'employee' is an Industrial Age hold-over that symbolizes one person working for another. The law still refers to 'masters' and 'servants', for crying out loud. I don't want people here working for me or anyone else. I want them here working for the mission and for their own personal fulfill-ment. So I'm proposing we use the word 'colleague' instead. My research says that 'Colleagues are those explicitly united in a common purpose and respecting each other's abilities to work toward that purpose.'[1] That's what I'm looking for here. Respect and common purpose.

"One other thing. I consider all of you to be professionals-I don't care what the outside world says about advanced education and credentials. Look at Jim Allen, who manages our packaging process, for example. Jim is an electro-mechanic with Navy ship experience, and one year of trade school. Yet he's in charge of over $5 million dollars of ultra-sophisticated packaging equip-ment, basically making all maintenance and operating decisions about his area—and dealing with the seasonal workforce. As far as I'm concerned, Jim's a professional in every sense of the word. You might even say he's the CEO of his own segment of the organization. There are probably some real CEOs that don't have the responsibility that Jim has. All of you are professional colleagues, and don't let anyone tell you otherwise." With a few exceptions, most in the room nodded with pride.

"The flattening of the organization, symbolized by the re-moval of titles, the elimination of command authority, including the unilateral authority to fire, and the designation of people as professional 'colleagues' rather than 'employees', will all serve to remove the perceived barriers to communication and help to drain politics from the ecosystem. At least that's my hope," Todd concluded.

"What's this about not being able to fire people?" Scott asked loudly. "How can we function unless we're able to get rid of the deadwood?"

---

1 http://www.reference.com/browse/colleague?qsrc=2890

"When did I say we wouldn't be able to get rid of the dead-wood?" Todd responded immediately. "Every organization needs to be able to exit people who no longer subscribe to the mission. Please note that I'm proposing to eliminate the unilateral authority to fire, not the authority to fire altogether. And we haven't gotten to it yet, but the manner in which people are fired is the subject of a whole other meeting." Scott shook his head querulously. Todd noted to himself that it was going to take a lot of selling to get Scott on board with the idea of self-management.

Todd walked over to the white board and contemplated it for several seconds. He had written **Self-Management**, followed by **Key Principles**, with arrows leading to **Keeping Commitments** and **No Use of Force**. To underscore his discussion points, he added **No Titles**, **No Command Authority**, and **No Unilateral Authority to Fire**. Finally, he wrote **Colleagues**. The first items on the list were identical to those he had conceived weeks before at his Santiam River cabin. "I think we've covered enough ground for one day," he said with a note of fatigue. "Let's meet next week and see where we're at on these concepts." Todd looked at the time, realized he was late for an advisory board meeting, and left. The cafeteria buzzed in animated discussion. The process had begun. Todd could not turn back now without suffering a severe loss of credibility.

Chapter Four: Challenges and Conflicts

∽

Todd greeted his advisory board members individually, thanking them for their ongoing support, and plopped into Sean Baker's nearest guest chair. He was eager to share his latest thoughts on self-management, as well as his impressions of the colleague meeting he'd just concluded.

Sean had gotten a heads-up about the colleague meeting and briefed Sandra and Bill (Todd had actually invited Sean to the meeting, but he felt that Todd should be the sole face of Berry-Way to its colleagues). After briefly describing the subject matter of the meeting to Sandra and Bill, Sean asked Todd how things had gone.

"OK, I think," Todd replied. "It's kind of hard to tell. There was a lot of content for one meeting, and a lot for the colleagues to digest. I'll give them a week or ten days to think it over, and then go back with some additional content. We'll just have to wait and see how well these things are accepted."

"Any outright objections?" Sandra asked.

"Well, there were some tough questions," Todd replied. "Scott couldn't seem to get his head around the notion of all colleagues being on the same level, with no one having command authority. He seemed to be conflating the idea of hierarchy with getting things done in the plant. I suppose that's a function of his background in traditional organizations."

"What about the other senior management staff?" asked Bill. "Did any other key leaders seem to have a problem with this approach?"

"Actually, they were pretty quiet," Todd replied. "Other than Scott, there seemed to be a lot of quiet contemplation. I assume people are trying to figure out how these changes will affect them—that's what I'd be doing in their shoes. Once they have a chance to digest the first meeting, there will probably be a lot more questions. I'll probably get nervous if there aren't."

"What's the next step, Todd?" asked Sandra. "How will you know when change is possible?"

"Here's my game plan," Todd responded. "Tell me what you think, and don't hold back any concerns. I don't have second chances to get this right. I've already started the ball rolling, and it's only going to pick up speed from here. So this is what I've got in mind.

"I've introduced the concept of self-management and it's key principles: keeping commitments and no use of force or coercion. There are several corollaries to these principles. One is that there is total organizational flatness with no hierarchy and no titles. The rejection of coercion means that no one has any command authority whatsoever. No one has the unilateral authority to fire anyone else. And everyone will be considered a colleague, not an employee. A true professional. And that goes for everyone from Scott Thorsen to the janitor—myself included. It's really kind of staggering when I think about it. I sincerely hope I know what I'm getting into, since there's no turning back now."

"Todd, are you saying that you are relinquishing the right to fire anyone, even though you're the owner of the company?" Bill asked incredulously.

"That's right, Bill," Todd replied. "This won't work if there's even one exception, even if that exception is the 'owner' of the company. It's all or nothing for me. These principles either work or they don't. We'll all soon find out just how well they work. And any organizational culture change needs a role model—I need to be that role model to show the way. There's no other approach to this, in my view."

"So how will you handle 'situations' where someone just needs to go, for performance reasons or otherwise?" Sean asked on behalf of the advisory board. "There must be a method for dealing with people when they are no longer positive contributors."

Todd had a ready answer. "I have thought about it, actually. I've devised a communication and dispute resolution process that can lead to the departure of a colleague when facts and circumstances require it. I'll e-mail you an outline of the process when I get back to my office."

With that, the board got down to discussing capital projects, strategy and succession planning. The next organizational change moves were up to Todd.

The following Monday morning, Todd met with Deborah to review some budget numbers for Steve Cameron. He asked for her honest appraisal of the company grapevine regarding his colleague meeting.

"I think people are intrigued, but struggling to get their heads around it," Deborah answered. "It's really tough to argue with the rationale, but you have to admit that most people aren't used to a work environment where there aren't any human bosses. It's just a cultural shift that people are taking some time getting used to."

"I think you've hit on something, Deborah," Todd said. "People are used to having a boss. And they do have bosses in a self-managed environment. They are their own bosses. And beyond that, the mission of the company is their boss—it should guide all their actions on behalf of the company. And even beyond that—each and every commitment that they make and the colleague to whom they make the commitment, is their boss for that commitment. So our colleagues will have more bosses than ever before under self-management. I just have to find a way to communicate that fact so it's understood.

"Deborah, can you ask Maria, Kyle, Mike, Teresa, Cathy and Scott if they can meet with me in the conference room at 1:00 p.m.?" Todd asked. "I've got to get some more unvarnished feedback on their insights into the reaction to our meeting the other day." Deborah nodded affirmatively. Todd always appreciated the fact that she always followed through on her commitments, and thought about how valuable that was to him.

At 1:00 p.m. sharp, Todd entered the conference room and greeted his most senior leaders. Taking a seat at the head of the table, he folded his hands in front of him on the table and looked around at each person, one by one. "I need your input," he said. "There isn't anything more important at this time than getting our organization and our culture right. I need your honest feedback about whether this is going to work or not. You don't have to disclose the names of people you've talked to about this. But I would like to know what the concerns are, if any, so I can be prepared for them when they come up."

Surprisingly, Scott spoke up first. "I'm having a hard time digesting your presentation from the other day," he said with a serious tone. "After thinking it over, and doing some reading on my own, I still can't come to the conclusion that the benefits of self-management outweigh the risks. Right now, I'm agnostic on self-management and need to hear more. And from what I'm hearing through the grapevine, I think most of the production technical leaders have concerns as well."

Todd thanked Scott for his comments, and made a mental note to spend some face time with him to plumb the depth of the production team's concern. "Thanks, Scott. I am worried about the production team's reaction. I appreciate your comments and promise to work hard to maintain your trust going forward. Anyone else?"

"I'm concerned about the Quality Control department," Maria offered. "They've been having small, closed meetings about these proposed changes, and I haven't been invited. One of my lab techs said that if they can't figure out who the boss is, they would rather work for a company that's more understandable. I don't totally understand their concerns, but suspect that the novelty of your ideas is a bit more than they want to deal with right now, Todd," she added. "I'm also concerned that Jill, our best lab technician, might be interested in the possibility of unionization."

The "U" word smacked Todd across the forehead with the full force of sudden recognition. Of course, he thought to himself. To borrow a physics metaphor, for every action, there is an equal and opposite reaction. If any colleague were to perceive his concept of self-management as a threat to their employment, whether justified or not, they might be persuaded to take drastic action. He made a mental note to call his labor attorney for advice, and seek some guidance from his advisory board as well. He had a list of "union do's and don'ts" stashed away from prior years. It was time to pull it out and dust it off, and get some good advice about how to proceed.

It was also gut-check time. While he could be justifiably concerned about the possibility of unionization, he had to summon the courage to go forward with his deeply held principles. He had already come this far. He would not be deterred from taking his organizational concepts all the way through to a conclusion.

Mike spoke next. "I think this is fabulous," he said. "Sales and marketing people are natural self-managers anyway. They don't need me to be their boss—they're already hard-wired to go out and make things happen. If anything, this will provide added motivation for them...I can't wait to see how they perform as self-managed professionals. And, obviously, I'm totally onboard with your ideas. At least, so far!"

Todd, beaming at Mike's enthusiasm, said, "Terrific! Can I join the sales team?" The group acknowledged his joke with laughter, and nodded appreciatively at Mike's declaration of support.

Todd looked at his remaining leadership team members. Teresa spoke next. "Self-management can only make my job easier," she said. "As long as I don't receive a pay cut, I couldn't be more enthusiastic about it. I love the idea of people taking care of their own people issues, rather than dumping them on HR!"

Kyle looked at Todd and shrugged as if to say 'Whatever'. "I don't see any effect on Acquisition one way or the other. We plan, we build relationships, and we buy fruits and vegetables. How will any of that change? I'll have to see more detail to know if your changes are good or not."

Kyle is going to present some major challenges to self-management, Todd thought to himself. "In the spirit of self-management,

Kyle, I'm going to look to you to determine exactly what detail you think you need, and where you intend to find it. Fair enough?" Todd asked. Kyle met his question with an awkward silence.

Cathy spoke up for Distribution. "No problems with the distribution team, as far as I can tell," she said. "We had a team meeting right after your presentation, and everyone was enthusiastic about self-management. The part about being a true professional really resonated with people. You can count on me to communicate with the team about this."

Todd smiled, and simply said, "Thank you very much, Cathy. Appreciate your support."

Todd glanced at Deborah, his closest confidant in the organization. "Well, Deborah, I guess we saved the best for last. What do you think?"

Deborah flashed a quick smile, understanding that Todd already knew the answer to his question. "The accounting staff is completely on board with self-management," she stated firmly. "And I think you know that I'd be happy to cheerlead the process. In my spare time, of course." The group chuckled, knowing that Deborah was famous for working sixty-hour weeks to get the numbers right.

"All right, team. I know you've got a lot of work to do today. I just wanted to get a quick flash report from you about the rather significant changes that we've been discussing. Thanks for your time and your candor. I'll have Deborah set up another all-hands meeting in the next week or so. We have some more ground to cover. Thanks again." With that, Todd stood up and quickly left the room. As he swiftly exited the conference room, he knew that there would be serious challenges ahead. But he was more convinced than ever that change was necessary.

The meeting began promptly at 8:00 a.m. with a full cafeteria and a rapt audience. Todd entered through the main door and stood in front of the white board, pen in hand.

Todd began with a hearty, "Good morning, everyone!" The group mumbled a "good morning" in response, some raising their coffee cups with a nod instead. "We've got some more ground to cover today, so I'd like to get started. Before we begin, are there any lingering questions from our last meeting?" Before Todd finished his sentence, a half-dozen hands were in the air. "OK, Cindy, what's on your mind?" he asked.

Cindy worked in distribution, and was one of the sharpest logisticians on the team. Whenever someone had a tough warehouse or inventory problem, she wrestled it to the ground faster than anyone. Todd appreciated the value she brought to the team and liked the fact that she was willing to ask questions. He also knew she had come over from a unionized warehouse operation and was used to a traditional hierarchical organization.

"I want to know how employees will be disciplined in the new system," she said. "If we have no human bosses, how will people be held accountable? How will people be let go? Unless, of course, your new system leads to some kind of Shangri-La, where all human beings magically become perfect performers." Todd had meant to speak to that very issue, and was pleased that Cindy's question gave him the perfect opening to do so.

"Great question, Cindy. One that's on a lot of minds, for sure. Let me start by asking a question: on a scale of one to ten, with ten being outstanding, how well does employee discipline work right now?" He paused while people thought about it. "How many would vote for a nine or ten?" No hands went up. "How about seven or eight?" A couple of hands went into the air. "Four to six?" The majority raised their hands. "Guess I need to ask this: how about one to three?" Once again, a couple of people raised their hands. "So very few of us think that our 'employee disciplinary' system works extremely well right now, right? It seems that we're pretty far from perfection right now. So I would be cautious about comparing the system that I have proposed, and that I'll detail further today, with perfection. Any new system, I would argue, shouldn't have to compete with perfection. It just has to be significantly better than what we have right now. And I hope that you'll give me a fair hearing about that as we go forward." Todd allowed his words to sink in, then added, "Thanks for your question, Cindy. Really appreciate it.

"To uphold colleague accountability: I propose a process for resolution of differences that is sound, considers the needs of all parties, and is designed to uphold the mission. But it requires a certain amount of courage on the part of all of you to make it work. It will take some guts. Again, this system may not be for everybody. But if you'll take the initiative to hold each other accountable, it has the potential to make us all happier and more prosperous," Todd observed.

"Here's how it would work. If anyone perceives any action on the part of a colleague that is not supportive of the mission, or is counterproductive to the work of other colleagues, he or she will be obligated to directly speak with that person about the issue. It's kind of like the military academy motto that 'we will not lie, cheat or steal nor tolerate those who do'. But I want you to keep in mind that we're not just talking about reprehensible conduct here. Any business issue that comes up, which, in the perception of any colleague, is counterproductive to the fulfillment of the mission, can and should be discussed with the other colleague as soon as possible.

"Speaking requires listening. It's always possible that the person perceiving an issue doesn't have all the facts, or is mistaken in their perceptions. So be it. That's why I'd like to have an initial face-to-face discussion. Get all the facts out and see if your perceptions are correct. See if you can resolve the issue up front. Remember, no one has any command authority in self-management. So if you'd like a course correction from a colleague, it has to be in the form of a request. Make a request! Be direct and tactful. Remember the golden rule: treat others the way you would like to be treated. Give the other person a chance to respond. By the way, if someone asks to speak to you about a work issue, do you have to listen to him or her? If you think you don't, I'd prefer you not work here. Everyone here has an obligation to communicate with each other, even with those with whom we rarely interface.

"If a colleague has a request made of them, they have a number of choices regarding how to deal with that request. First, they can agree to fulfill the request and change course.

Assuming they keep that commitment—remember the first key principle?—there isn't much more to discuss. Or they can suggest a compromise that makes everyone happy. The third option, declining to fulfill the request, is trickier. Now the requesting colleague has to make a choice. If, after face-to-face discussion, that person is still convinced that the request is necessary, he or she has an obligation to bring in a third party mediator. This will be another colleague specially trained in mediation, to help resolve the differences between the two. And guess what? The colleague of whom the request was made has an obligation to participate in the mediation—simply by virtue of being a colleague at this company and agreeing to self-manage.

"Now let's say that the colleagues have discussed the issue with a third party and still haven't agreed on a solution. What then? I'm proposing that we use a panel of colleagues, no more than six, to sit down with both parties and reach a resolution. We will have our trained mediators also trained to facilitate, and they will keep the discussion on track and make sure all relevant facts are heard. My hope is that this step is extremely rare and that most issues are cleared up before they get that far. But...if they don't, we will definitely have a process in place to deal with it."

"What happens if the panel or jury or whatever splits down the middle," Cindy asked. "Isn't there a risk of deadlock here?"

"Great question, Cindy. I appreciate you bringing that up. Let's think about this for a moment. If we call our new ecosystem self-management, and we have banned force and coercion, how should this panel make decisions?" Todd asked the group.

"Sounds like a jury to me," Scott offered. "Majority vote should decide."

"Any other thoughts?" Todd asked.

"Here's what I think," offered Deborah. "I think that the panel should have no more power to force a solution than anyone else. No force or coercion means no force or coercion. Even if the panelists unanimously agree with the requesting party, the other person doesn't have to agree."

Todd smiled to himself, grateful that Deborah had come to his rescue so the idea wouldn't have to come from him. "I think that's right, Deborah. No force means no force. Persuasion, influence: great. But no force allowed. Period."

"OK, so the parties still can't agree after meeting with a panel. Then what?" Scott asked, with frustration in his voice.

"Then I'll join the panel," Todd offered. "And we'll start from scratch, and have a relentless and thorough exploration of the facts and how the facts relate to the mission. I'm pretty good at influence and persuasion, and I care about the mission—a lot. So the final step is that both parties get to set down with me as an additional panelist, and I'll facilitate and serve as the guardian of the mission. If the facts are still unclear after I get done exploring them, so be it. But if the facts are clear, then I'll make sure the colleagues understand them. And we'll stay in the conversation until its conclusion. I want to make the cost of avoidance and obfuscation so high that colleagues will avoid any temptation to go there, and instead make every effort to achieve a successful resolution."

"Sounds like coercion to me," Scott asserted.

"You're entitled to your opinion, of course," Todd replied. "But again, no system is going to be perfect. Human beings aren't perfect. At least I haven't come across any perfect people lately. Remember: to replace our current traditional system, we don't have to come up with a theoretically perfect system, since no such system exists. We just have to come up with something that is significantly better than what we have now.

"And I recall from our first meeting that no one raised their hand when I asked whether they wanted to be told what to do every day by a superior. I think you all know your own jobs, right? Anyone change their mind about that since our last meeting?" Hearing no response, and expecting none, Todd felt a surge of confidence that his message was taking hold, at least for the majority of colleagues.

"I'd like to hear an example of how this would work," Scott added, with a slight trace of disbelief in his voice.

Todd reflected for a few seconds, and snapped his fingers. "Okay, let's work through an example. Suppose one of our lab techs is transiting the process area and sees a foreign material-

FM-, say motor oil, dripping into the filling process along with our product being filled. It's the night shift, and I'm on a business trip back East. How would this be handled right now?"

"She would get ahold of me, whether I'm on site or not, for an analysis of the situation and I would take definitive action," Scott replied.

"And you would do a great job fixing the problem, I have no doubt," Todd responded. "But it might take some time to get ahold of you. Let's say for the sake of argument that you're at home and at least an hour away. And we run 4,000 cases per hour. So even an hour's lost production would harm our contribution margin. Here's how I envision things happening."

Todd wrote on the white board: **Step One: Face-to-Face Discussion**. "In a self-managed accountability process," Todd continued, "our lab technician, call her Katie, has every right-and in fact, obligation-to walk right up to the filler operator and communicate her concern, and request action to resolve the urgent situation on the spot. Let's say her request is to shut the line down immediately while Scott is notified, and Quality Control can analyze product samples to determine the problem scope. Is there a pre-determined response from the filler operator? No. He-call him Adam-has every right to accept her request. He may reject her request. Or they may reach a compromise—perhaps he shuts the line down after notifying other departments downstream in the process. In any event, he has an absolute obligation, consistent with safety, to listen sincerely to the request and respond honestly based on facts and circumstances.

"Let's say Adam hears the facts from Katie, realizes that she's right, and honors her request. We've just saved ourselves a huge problem. On the other hand, let's say Adam convinces Katie that what she saw wasn't really going into the product, and production continues. Again, we've just saved ourselves a huge problem. But let's say Katie is right, and Adam just won't compromise or agree. Now Katie has an obligation to bring in a mediator, as quickly as possible, given the risks. Our standard operating procedures require her to notify you, Scott, as soon as possible. So while Katie is arranging mediation, you are already on the way here from home-again, at least an hour away.

"Adam has already agreed to the accountability process by virtue of being a colleague of BerryWay. So when the designated mediator arrives, within the next ten minutes or so, Adam knows that he needs to have his facts straight. So he studies the situation a little bit harder, realizes that his conclusions may have been hasty, and then goes into the mediation session. After a few pointed questions from the mediator, Adam concludes that he cannot dispute Katie's observation, and concedes the point, shutting down the line. We've only lost a third as much product as we would have if you were an hour away and we were depending on you to make a decision.

"But Adam may be stubborn, or suffer from cognitive dissonance, or whatever," Todd continued. "So it's possible that he just willfully ignores evidence and stonewalls the mediator. Now Katie can start the colleague panel process with help from one of our facilitation colleagues. Obviously, that's going to take some time, and we've already burned up half an hour or so. But if Katie's right and sticks to her guns, she'll continue with the process. While that process is going on, it's likely that you've already arrived and taken control of the situation, Scott. And when, not if, you discover that Adam was negligent in allowing the FM in the product, and in stonewalling Katie throughout the accountability process, then you'll probably be having a much more serious request for Adam which will start the process all over again. And it may be along the lines of requesting that he conclude his services to BerryWay." Todd couldn't help noticing the perplexed look on Scott's face, and asked for any further questions. Hearing none, he pressed forward.

"So that's the Accountability Process that I'm proposing," Todd explained, as he wrote the words **Accountability Process** on the white board. "We jumped ahead a little bit but it was something that I wanted to cover anyway, so that's okay. Again, I'd like you to think about this for a few days and then come back with any questions or concerns. The idea isn't to drop this on your heads, all at once. The idea is to communicate and explain and then communicate some more until all questions and concerns are addressed. With me so far?" Seeing heads nodding yes, he continued to the next topic.

"The next element of a self-managed environment is what I'll call a **Coaching and Mentoring Culture**". Writing the words on the white board, Todd began. "Anyone know what I'm talking about here?"

Maria raised her hand and said, "I think it has to do with helping each other grow and perform on the job. I can't think of any other description for it."

"You couldn't be more right, Maria," Todd responded. That's exactly what I'm talking about here. By the way, does anyone know what corporate culture means, exactly?" The room remained quiet. "Here's what I think it means." He took up the white board pen. "I think it has to do with shared assumptions about work and the workplace. Assumptions you may not even be consciously aware of. For example, does anyone here work a strict forty-hour workweek?" The cafeteria twittered with laughter. "You've got to be kidding," Mike interjected. "We all work at least forty-eight and sometimes a lot more."

"That's a good example, Mike," Todd noted. "Everyone here sustains some pretty significant work hours, especially in the summertime. Why do we do that, and not just knock off after our eight hours are up?" he asked.

"Because we would simply fail," declared Cathy. "If our team has an order to get out to a warehouse right before quitting time, you can bet we'll put that order ahead of everything else. It's pretty clear to all of us that customers pay the bills, and make our jobs possible. To not serve the customer would just be unthinkable. Especially for the distribution team, which gets all the customer complaints."

"Great comment, Cathy," Todd said. "What are some other aspects of our culture at BerryWay?"

"How about camaraderie and esprit de corps?" Deborah asked. "It seems like we have a pretty great group of cooperative people here, and we're usually trying to do the best thing for our stakeholders. And usually, people seem pretty happy to be here."

"Sounds good, Deborah. Anything else?"

Todd spent the next fifteen minutes with the group coming up with a list of BerryWay's cultural aspects. When the group finished, this is the list they came up with:

Dedication
Willingness to work long hours
Helpfulness
Trust
Camaraderie
Integrity
Honesty
Open communication
Diversity of opinion
Respect
Sensitivity to feelings
Enthusiasm
Difficult conversations avoided
Conflicts unaddressed

"So as you look at this table, what cultural aspects would you like to see more of, and which would you like to see less of?" Todd asked the group.

"Well, it's pretty obvious that we'd like to see more of everything except the two on the bottom," Maria replied. "I'd like to think that most everyone agrees with me."

"Thanks, Maria. Good point. Now: are there any aspects of culture that we don't currently have that you would appreciate seeing in our workplace?" Todd continued.

"Well, I'd like to see more flexibility," Kyle noted. "It doesn't make sense to require us to be physically present in the factory when we can be just as productive, or even more productive, working from home."

"You're right, Kyle," Todd admitted. "I've always been a bit biased in favor of physical presence in the workplace, because of the need for constant communication among colleagues. But for the sake of argument, let's start a list going and I pledge to you that I'm committed to making this the best possible workplace for everybody."

For the next several minutes, the group brainstormed the cultural aspects that they would like to cultivate at BerryWay. This is the list they came up with:

Flexibility
Focus on professional development and career paths
Stronger leadership throughout company
Stronger teamwork
Accountability
Mentoring
Closer linkage of departments (fewer silos)

"Great list, people," Todd said appreciatively. "This gives us a good direction to go in. Now we have some things to strengthen, some things to eliminate, and some things to adopt. Another question about culture: what are some artifacts of our culture?" Todd wanted to find out how observant his colleagues were.

"We have an open-books policy, thanks to you and Deb," Maria noted. "That seems like an indicator of our cultural aspect of open communication."

"Right you are, Maria," Todd said. "Anyone else?"

"Well, right along with open books are open doors," noted Scott. "Unless there's some kind of personnel matter going on, or a meeting with Steve Cameron or some regulatory officials, everyone's always got an open door. Of course, that can be a giant productivity killer if you're trying to get some work out and someone wants to tell the latest political joke.

"Here's another one: we only have this one cafeteria for all employees—excuse me—colleagues; whether seasonal or salaried," Scott continued. "And only one set of washrooms. And our administrative and sales offices are right next to the factory floor. I think that symbolizes a sort of egalitarianism, myself."

"How about bloodshot eyes as an artifact of hard work?" Cathy piped up to laughter.

"Good. I think you get the idea of culture," Todd said. "I want you to understand this because what I'd like to propose as a support system for self-management is the adoption of a coaching and mentoring culture. I'd like everyone here to have access to coaching services, both to improve your effectiveness at work and to help figure out your career path and relationships. I've gotten up to speed on the payback from coaching—and it's phenomenal. And I'd like to adopt a formal mentoring program for all new hires, beginning as soon as possible. There's no reason new colleagues should have to try and figure out their job, a new culture, and fifty new teammates all at the same time. I also want to train all of you to be coaches within the workplace, so you can help each other in a positive way. My idea is to use a coaching and mentoring culture to do three things: one, help people become more effective; two, support and assist self-management, and three; fix the things in the culture that you want fixed. We already have an excellent culture; but it's not as good as it could be. There's no reason we can't make it better. Culture is strong and powerful. I'd like to harness it to our goals and make it work for us and not against us. How does that sound so far?"

The silence in the cafeteria was broken only by the omnipresent hum of the vending machine motors.

"Thanks for sticking with this for two meetings now," Todd said, taking a swig of bottled water to clear his throat. "Just have a few more concepts to cover. One big one, actually. Let's take a fifteen-minute break and come back and continue."

As the people in the room scattered to grab donuts and coffee, or catch up on voicemails, Todd turned to Deborah and asked, "How do you think this is going so far?"

She replied, "Hard to read minds, but they were certainly engaged. You had a lot of participation in your culture brainstorms. Saw a lot of heads nodding up and down—I think you were making your points very well. But I'm concerned about Scott. When I think about his comments in the leadership meeting earlier, and his objections to the accountability process, I just feel that he's not embracing self-management."

"I know what you mean, Deborah," Todd replied. "I've got some work to do with him. With no guarantee of the results, I might add." He was resigned to the possibility that not everyone would be on board with the concept of self-management, and told himself that was okay in the long run. The short run could inflict some pain, however.

"I'm also interested in Kyle's reaction," Deborah told him. "He doesn't seem to be engaged at all. It's strange, like he's not even in the meeting."

Todd pursed his lips, thinking but not responding. It was time to finish the meeting.

"Okay, let's hit the last few topics of the day," Todd said, writing the word **Freedom** on the white board. "Who wants to take a crack at why this might be important, desirable, necessary for self-management?"

"Because it's the only way to satisfy the deepest desires of the human heart to create, to give value to others, to leave a legacy," Teresa volunteered. "It's the way human beings are wired. We want to have a say in what we do. No one knows our job better than we do. And we should have a great deal of freedom to responsibly seek to better ourselves and others at work."

The room was stunned into complete silence as colleagues turned and looked at Teresa. Everyone respected her intelligence and warmth, but few had any idea of the depth of her wisdom. The silence held in the room for several seconds before Todd broke it.

"Thanks, Teresa. I don't think anyone could have said it better than that. I think there are some very practical benefits to freedom at work as well," Todd said. "Let's take a company that practices real self-management with responsible freedom. What if one of our janitors had loads of ambition, and studied thermodynamics and mathematics at night school, and talked to the electro-mechanics on breaks and lunches about our equipment? Call him James. Let's say he studied and talked, and talked and studied, for three or four years.

"Fast forward four years later, and James has enough technical knowledge that he's able to suggest a processing line reconfiguration that increases throughput by forty percent. He creates a project proposal, sells it internally, backs it up with facts and data, and gets me to approve it—and it works great! Now James moves into an electro-mechanic position.

"As an electro-mechanic, he studies the other parts of the business. He goes to night school and learns logistics, accounting, sales and marketing, human resources, IT. He spends time in the field and learns the acquisition process backward and forward. He takes leadership classes, and eventually gets accepted into the local MBA program. He volunteers for almost every colleague workgroup and committee, as well as customer visits.

"After a few years of study, excelling as an electro-mechanic and as a newly-minted MBA, he comes up with a strategic plan to start up an entirely new business with an entirely new line of products with new markets. He backs up the plan with unassailable facts and data, and sells it to key prospective stakeholders, beginning with me. It has the potential to exceed BerryWay revenues and drive even higher profit margin. James and I convince Steve Cameron to loan us the construction capital and operating lines to start up a new company.

"Here's my question: who am I going to pick to run the new company?" Todd asked rhetorically, knowing that his colleagues already knew the answer.

"In an environment of freedom, you know how to do your own job better than anyone else-and you should be free to make it better. In an environment of freedom, you should be able to talk to anyone in the enterprise about anything having to do with the enterprise. In an environment of freedom, there should be absolutely no barriers to pursuing your mission and the mission of the enterprise to the best of your ability. And finally, in a free environment, there should be no barriers to any of you becoming whatever you wish to be," Todd concluded. "I want to see a workplace where anyone can achieve their dreams, whatever they may be, regardless of position."

"Well, if it's not good enough for them here, they're already free," Scott opined. "They're free to quit!" A smattering of attendees chuckled at the comment. "Why would anyone need more freedom than that?" Scott continued.

Todd locked eyes with Scott and replied slowly and firmly. "Because freedom in the workplace is the most efficient, effective and profitable way to operate. And because it's the way people really live in their own personal lives." he said simply.

"Let's break and come back at one o'clock...there are a few more things to discuss, then we'll be done for the day, I promise."

While grabbing a sandwich and coffee with Deborah and Mike, Todd's cell phone began to buzz. He picked it up and listened for a moment, muttered "Thanks," and looked at it and then at his companions. "That was Kyle," he said with a tone of resignation in his voice. "He just quit, along with three of his field department aces. Looks like we're getting a reaction to our self-management meetings. And Teresa will have to recruit another team leader."

Todd started the meeting with the news, telling the assembled colleagues that Kyle had chosen to no longer be a part of the team. An uncomfortable silence fell on the room, reminding people that they were about some very serious business with significant repercussions for their work lives. It was obvious to all that Kyle was not engaged with the self-management discussion and had shown no enthusiasm for the process whatsoever. For him to quit mid-day during a company meeting was a bit discomfiting to most of the colleagues who worked with him. It would be interesting to see how the grapevine handled the news in the next forty-eight hours, Todd thought to himself. He also realized that no matter how much cheerleading he did for the idea of self-management, not everyone was going to see things his way. Every individual would have a different calculus regarding the advantages and disadvantages.

"There are a few more things I want to put on the table before calling it a day," Todd noted. "First of all, I want to know how all of you relate to the BerryWay mission." He had formulated the company mission himself when he started the company, without input from anyone. Now it was time to find out if it resonated with the colleagues. There were plaques hanging throughout the facility displaying the mission—if it wasn't written in the minds and hearts of the colleagues working there it wasn't worth anything.

Todd held up one of the company mission plaques: 'Our mission is to produce Willamette Valley-sourced food products that delight customers throughout North America and the world.' "So how does this work for you?" he asked the group. "Does it inspire you to come to work every day?" Some embarrassed laughter ensued. "Most of you were hired with a job description that contained the mission," he continued. "What did you think about it then?"

"I thought it was great," Mike chimed in. "It was something that motivated me and attracted me to this company. I actually read it every day, and think about it when I'm talking to customers. We actually joke about it, as in, 'what can I do to delight you today'."

"Okay, that's good," Todd replied. "But here's what I'd like to do. Since we're starting a new era here, I'd like new eyes to consider the mission—a workgroup of self-managed volunteers, if you will. The mission is vital in self-management–it answers the questions 'why do we exist?', 'why are we here?' and 'what is our purpose?'. I think the mission should guide the actions of each one of us, and play a vital role in conflict resolution. It should also express our value to our stakeholders. That's how important the mission is. Any volunteers to look at the mission?"

Todd saw several hands shoot up, including those of Teresa and Mike. He was pleased with the response. "Thank you. As you can see who else has volunteered, please meet together and see what you can come up with for us.

"The mission, besides being our lodestar, can keep us out of trouble," Todd continued. "Most of us aren't old enough to remember President Eisenhower, right? Does anyone know what his big job was prior to becoming president?" Silently thanking his high school history teacher, and seeing no hands, he continued. "He had a rather impressive title on his business card: Supreme Allied Commander — how about that for a title? And he had a clear mission–simple to articulate, hard to fulfill. His mission was simply this: enter the European continent and destroy the army of the Third Reich. President Roosevelt promised him unlimited resources in order to accomplish the mission, but fulfillment of the mission was up to him.

"There were many distractions along the way, from allies and enemies alike—but Ike stuck to his mission. He poured his heart and soul into it, and was ultimately successful. It's one of the best examples of achieving success through crystal clear mission focus.

"Why do you come to work here every day? If the answer isn't immediately clear to you, then it's time to start thinking about the mission, and about your own personal mission," Todd concluded. "Can we have the mission workgroup begin meeting right away and report back to us next month?" The volunteers nodded affirmation.

"Self-management will also require a set of core values and principles," Todd continued. "We've already covered a conflict resolution process, and that will be one of the principles. But we'll need more that that to bring self-management alive. So what are our values here?"

"Wouldn't they naturally follow the things we want to see in our culture, that we've already identified?" asked Teresa. "It seems like they're basically the same."

"Good point," Todd replied. "Let's capture a few and see how they shake out. What are our core values here?"

Todd wrote while colleagues shouted out their thoughts. This is the list they came up with:

Initiative
Teamwork
Dedication
Helpfulness
Trust
Fun
Integrity
Honesty
Openness
Tolerance
Caring
Finding Opportunity in Conflict
Enthusiasm
Flexibility
Accountability
Superior Efficiency and Effectiveness
Highly Innovative
Win-Win Agreements

"Who was it that suggested 'win-win agreements,' again?" Todd inquired. David, a junior logistics colleague, tentatively raised his hand. "Could you explain why that's important?" Todd asked.

"Well, if an agreement isn't structured to be at least competitive with each person's other options, or it favors one person over the other, it creates insecurity. One person will always be looking for the exit ramp. And it hurts their relationship. Good agreements always have to be win-win to work in the long run," David concluded.

"Excellent observation, David," Todd replied. "I'm suggesting you participate in the workgroup I'm about to request."

"Cathy, you came up with 'finding opportunity in conflict'. What did you mean by that?" Todd queried.

"Well, if you look at the Chinese symbol for conflict, it consists of two characters," she replied. "One character represents danger—to the relationship, to the team, perhaps to the enterprise itself. The other character represents opportunity, a chance to make things even better than they were before. And I happen to believe that conflict is inevitable—you simply can't run a family, much less a company—without conflict. The 'make-or-break' for people involved in conflict is how the conflict is handled. Poorly handled, not good. Handled well so that all interests are accounted for, an opportunity. That's what I meant."

"That's terrific, Cathy," Todd said appreciatively. "Thanks for sharing. Now here's my final request of the day. Can we have some volunteers get together over the next month and craft a statement of values and principles that incorporates the accountability process?" This time, more hands shot up than Todd could count. The process was starting to engage people. Todd was still worried whether there were more Kyles in the group looking for an exit ramp. But for now, the enthusiasm and interest in self-management was starting to build.

"Here's my suggestion," Todd said with a smile. "In the spirit of true self-management, I'm going to suggest that whoever is interested in crafting a statement of values and principles over the next month engage with other self-managers here to voluntarily come together and make it happen!

"You'll be hearing soon about some tools and techniques that I've been working on to facilitate self-management. We'll need to have agreements in place between each other, so we know what to expect from each other in terms of information flow and results. Call them 'Colleague Accountability Agreements' for now. And we'll need Key Performance Indicators to measure and track performance ourselves, since we won't have bosses to do it for us. But you'll get more information on those things later. That's all I've got for now, we'll meet next month and continue the process. Thanks for participating today."

"One more question before we leave," Scott stood up and addressed Todd firmly. "You seem to be suggesting that we're breaking new ground here. I guess I still don't see what the big deal is. At my last company, we had an employee empowerment program that seemed to work well. The suggestion boxes filled up more than ever, and people seemed to be happier, at least for a while. What's the difference between what we're doing and employee empowerment?"

Anticipating this comment, Todd was confidently prepared. "Because, Scott, the term 'employee empowerment' implies that one person is transferring power to another person. In the real world, what is given can be taken away. In self-management, colleagues already have all the power they need to make anything happen they want to have happen from the moment they start work. Self-management is beyond empowerment. Self-management is power itself." Without waiting for a response, Todd thanked the group again, and left quickly.

Chapter Five: Arrows for the Quiver

❧

The following Monday, Todd met again with his advisory board. They were eager to find out about the progress of self-management at BerryWay. Todd and Sarah had been able to get away for the weekend and escape the pressure cooker of business responsibilities. Now Todd felt the need to unload to his team of advisors and get their wisdom on implementation.

"So how's it going, Todd?" asked Sandra with a smile. "I see that shipments to Synergy hit an all-time high last month. You have a great reputation in our boardroom, that's for sure. And the quality has been superb. Looks like you're really hitting on all cylinders."

"Well, I wish I could be sanguine, Sandra," Todd replied. "I feel just okay about the way we're hitting our business targets. I have a nagging and well-justified feeling that we're not doing as well as we could be, however."

"How is the idea of self-management going over with your employees—I mean, colleagues, Todd?" asked Sean, looking serious. "That's a pretty big change. Is everyone on board?"

"I can't honestly say everyone is on board, Sean," replied Todd. "I just can't tell for sure. I'm pretty sure that my production leader, Scott, is not getting it. And you heard about Kyle already," referring to his departed acquisition manager. "Even though Kyle left with three other managers, I'm confident that Teresa will be able to find an excellent replacement. In fact, she's talking to several candidates right now. Sure was great to have those rigorous competency models and job descriptions ready. So I think the business risk there is minimal. We have enough time before the season to get this squared away.

"I will say this. I felt a definite momentum shift in favor of the concept of self-management at our last colleague meeting. We had a lot of volunteers offer to help craft the mission and vision statements. I took that as a very positive sign."

"I do have one very serious concern, however," Todd continued. "The grapevine is humming to the effect that there is a unionization campaign going on. Can't say for sure who's involved, it may have originated in the quality control department. Just one more headache to deal with, as if trying to change the entire culture and mindset of the company weren't enough." Todd's bloodshot eyes and weary demeanor betrayed the extra hours he'd been putting in trying to drive home the benefits of self-management.

Bill, who had been listening quietly, finally spoke up. "I know exactly what it's like to go through a campaign," he said. "I've got a phone number for an excellent law firm for you. You need to get up to speed, along with your key leaders-anyone who could be considered a 'supervisor' under the law, so that you don't hand the union any ammunition. You have to do things right. When all is said and done, if you communicate your message properly, you should be in good shape. It's just too bad this had to come while you're trying to implement change." Todd managed a half-smile of gratitude for Bill and thanked him for the advice.

Following Bill's discussion with Todd, the parties lapsed into a two-hour conversation regarding audits, recruitment and financial matters. "Any other thoughts for me before I head back into battle?" Todd finally leaned back and asked.

"Just one," Sean offered. "Now that you're in it up to your eyeballs, don't quit or slow down. Go full speed ahead, or you'll get so bogged down that everything sinks. We're counting on you to do a great job, Todd. Best of luck and don't hesitate to call for help." Todd nodded, thanked his board appreciatively, and went back to work.

༄

The following Monday, Todd met Deborah at her desk. "We're coming up on the next colleague meeting to discuss self-management," he noted. "And with all my networking and study, I've come to the conclusion that we're missing a few arrows in the quiver. We need to put some resources in place so that people can self-manage effectively. And I'd really like to bounce stuff off you and the other leaders here so we don't put out ideas that are half-baked. I'd like them to be at least three-quarters baked," he offered with a wry smile.

"What did you have in mind, Todd?" Deborah queried.

"I think we need to create a workplace ecology that replicates, as much as possible, the feeling of actual business ownership. I'm the 'owner', and yet I don't really own anything, if you think about it. The bank holds the long-term capital debt, and I'm just the designated steward of the capital for the time being. If I fail to produce a return on this capital, eventually society will take these assets away and give them to someone else who can produce a return. I can no more leave and go do something else than that fire hydrant in front of the driveway. I have personal guarantees to lenders, personal commitments to colleagues, not to mention my passion for creating an amazing company. I'm not complaining, really. I love what I do. I really think that our colleagues, if they can experience some of the same economic and legal rigor that I face every day, will be in a much better position to self-manage and create prosperity and happiness for themselves.

"Here's what I'd like you to do over the next week, Deborah," he continued. "Get with Heather Kay, our business attorney, and work with her to draft a simple document—not more than a few pages—that we'll title 'Colleague Accountability Agreement'. It's what I mentioned the other day in the meeting. I want every colleague to have an explicit agreement outlining his or her 'deal' as a colleague at BerryWay. When our workgroup comes up with the final mission, vision and principles, I want those to be included in this agreement. I also want every colleague to have an *individual* mission, completely aligned with the enterprise mission, so that every person here has absolutely no doubt about why they are here and what results they are expected to deliver. I also want to list the business processes they are responsible for, in excruciating detail, along with any measures of performance that we can attach to them."

Todd spent the next hour laying out for Deborah what he was looking for in the Colleague Accountability Agreement, confident that she would come back with a superb result in a timely fashion. He made a mental note to give her a performance increase as soon as possible. He was willing to pay a premium for proven reliability. It was worth so much, especially now.

The following week, Deborah met with Todd and laid out the draft agreement that she and Heather Kay had cooked up with Todd's direction. This is what they created:

DRAFT

Colleague Accountability Agreement (CAA)

The purpose of this agreement is to define the relationship between _____, and his/her fellow colleagues of BerryWay, Inc., in order to improve the well-being and prosperity of all.

I, _____, hereby agree to wholeheartedly, in good faith and without reservation, commit in total to the BerryWay mission, vision and principles, as well as my own Individual Mission. I agree to be responsible for all activities that enter my scope of professional awareness.

Company Mission: TBD

Company Values and Principles: TBD

Colleague's Individual Mission: TBD

I agree to assume ownership for the following business processes, key performance indicators (KPIs), decision rights, resources and requirements for information distribution:

_____

I require the following resources to effectively perform my Individual Mission:

_____

I understand that I have the full authority and responsibility to initiate the acquisition, as needed, or termination of services of other colleagues pursuant to the colleague accountability process.

I agree to pursue a program of continuous learning, and to share the results of that professional learning with other colleagues. I anticipate additional learning in the following areas:

_____

I agree to personally notify fellow colleagues of any perceived legal, regulatory, product, or human safety risk, or any other prospective threat to the safety or security of colleagues, without delay.

I represent that I possess the required ability, talent, education, experience and skill to perform my agreed-upon responsibilities.

I commit to the following professional goals and objectives:

_____

I understand that if I wish to conclude my services to BerryWay, that I may negotiate a financial bridge of from three to six months, whereby I may receive full pay while seeking another economic situation, so long as my departure is voluntary and I remain a colleague in good standing, and so long as I am willing to continue to render services at a level that maintains reasonable continuity within my area of professional contribution.

Signed: _____

Dated: _____

Colleagues:

_____

_____

_____

_____

⁓

The following day, Maria knocked on Todd's office door. "Can we talk for a minute?" she asked.

"Of course," Todd replied, "What's on your mind?"

"As you probably remember, there was a bit of buzz around a possible organizing campaign that we discussed at our last leader meeting," she recalled. "I've been hearing a few comments around the lab that the pay is too low relative to the workload. I just thought that you should know about it."

"Okay. Thanks, Maria. I'll fit it onto the plate with everything else that's going on!" Todd replied with a pained smile. There was something brewing, but there were also ramifications for self-management. He would get to the compensation questions later. First, he told himself, there were other questions to address.

⁓

Todd had been thinking about how to provide feedback in a self-managed ecosystem. In a traditional hierarchy, there were bosses and managers and supervisors and all manner of superiors around to tell people how well they are doing. In self-management, each individual would have to be able to gauge his or her own performance and adjust accordingly. Actually, self-management should theoretically provide much better feedback, since fifty colleagues—and even more during the production season—would have full authority to question any activity in the enterprise, even strategy. Todd made a mental note to himself that he really wasn't advocating an elimination of structure. What he was doing was replacing an inefficient, brittle structure with one that was far more fluid and dynamic—and effective.

There was no way that one boss could provide the same degree of oversight and leadership that a self-managed enterprise could provide. The odds of a single boss or manager catching a person doing something wrong were probably less than one in ten. The odds of a responsible colleague observing a problem, however, were very high. So long as colleagues had the gumption to challenge one another to better performance, Todd had no doubt which environment was superior. Responsible people with initiative, integrity, competence and passion could cause other people to change for the better. Those were the kinds of people with whom Todd wanted to associate. He was tired of hearing excuses in the workplace when things didn't go well. Excuses had no value to him. The only reason to investigate why things went wrong was to figure out how to avoid failure in the future. In too many cases, it appeared to Todd, failure led to recrimination instead of learning. Too often, small issues had festered until becoming major headaches, sometimes even workplace cancers requiring him to wield his scalpel of authority. He wanted to remove the excuses for non-performance, and the ability to hide behind excuses. He wanted each and every colleague to assume total responsibility for the business results of the enterprise. There were a lot of good people performing well at BerryWay. Todd wanted them to soar even higher.

Todd also savored the idea of freedom at work. To the degree that colleagues faced few constraints in seeking better ways of working, there would be more passion, innovation, and continuous improvement. He smiled at the thought of having fewer constraints to high performance than anywhere else in the commercial world. To be a maverick, a groundbreaker, was inspiring. He loved the idea of natural coordination around a common mission. Multiplying strong individual talent by rigorous individual effort and a high degree of coordination would create powerful business results, benefiting everyone in the enterprise. He wanted to work with people with passion, willing to put in the intensive time necessary to drive performance. He knew that if people didn't love what they were doing, they wouldn't perform very well or for very long. And if they didn't love working in an environment that gave them complete freedom to innovate and execute, they probably wouldn't last very long at BerryWay. Todd thought about Kyle, and how Kyle's silence during all the self-management discussions spoke volumes in hindsight. This wouldn't be everyone's cup of tea. People who needed constant direction and prodding wouldn't last in this environment. Nor would people who needed to exercise authority. It was going to be a bumpy ride.

Todd was fully aware that self-management would be messy in the short term, but extraordinarily powerful and elegant in the long term. Self-management, grounded on solid principles requiring voluntary association, would increase power and leverage over business results. Every interaction or trade between two self-managed individuals would leave both parties better off, in pursuit of the enterprise mission and their own personal prosperity. So long as interactions are voluntary, the result is always abundance. Todd smiled to himself again, envisioning the future. It looked bright.

He needed to come up with a way for people to measure their own performance, and be aware of the performance of others. He made a note to call his leadership team together that afternoon.

At 1:00 p.m. sharp, his leaders met in the conference room. There was an empty seat where Kyle usually sat, and it made the group feel a little uncomfortable. "How's the search going for Kyle's replacement?" Todd asked Teresa.

"Fairly well," she replied. "We're down to three candidates now. I should have interviews scheduled by the end of this week. I'm glad we did all that work up front with the competency models."

"Okay, here's what I want to discuss, and I don't want to keep you long, because you're all as busy as I am," Todd started out. "You heard me mention Key Performance Indicators the other day. We have to propose a way of tracking individual performance if self-management is to have any hope of succeeding here. What suggestions do you have for feedback of accurate, objective performance data?"

Mike opened up the discussion. "Here's what we did in my previous company. Every job was assigned a Key Performance Indicator. They called them 'KPIs'. Some jobs had several KPIs, some had very few. They were usually represented by graphs—

simple x/y axis stuff, and laid out visually how well we were performing. The graphs were posted on our 'KPI wall' so results
were visible to everyone. We referred to them as our 'score-
boards'. Those were the hard numbers that you had to live with
at compensation time. They basically told the story of how well
you performed. Of course, some people shared responsibility
for certain processes, and it wasn't always easy to break out individual performance. But we had another system to try and address that question."

"What was that?" Cathy asked, curiously.

"There was a 360-degree evaluation," Mike continued. "The
KPIs took care of all the hard, objective data: sales per month,
average price per case, that kind of thing. But the 360 took a lot
of subjective stuff into account: communication skills, sensitiv-
ity, adaptability, and things like that. The explanation was that
while the KPIs could measure items that were easy to measure,
the 360-degree evaluation took into account the thousands of
observations that your peers have of you throughout the year.
They used it for development purposes, I believe, and not for
compensation. But it was another source of great feedback.
Some people were quite surprised by the results."

Todd went around the room and solicited the experiences
of key influencers regarding feedback systems. Thanking them
appreciatively, he left the meeting, grabbed some books, and
headed for his home office.

He couldn't help remembering that one of the top items on
the list of core values from the colleagues was fun. It occurred to
him that whatever measurement and feedback system he came
up with, it would have to promote fun. He didn't want people
running around spraying each other with seltzer bottles, but he
did want people focused like laser beams on superior execution,
using feedback for constant improvement. He wanted to obliterate the distinction between work and play. He wanted work to
be fun.

The following day, he convened another team meeting.
"We've always had some measures of performance around here,"
he noted, holding up a copy of the daily output report. "The

monthly financials are another example of performance reporting. My request is that you survey all the jobs in your respective areas, beginning with your own jobs. Think about the results you're responsible for. Then ask yourself: 'how do I know if I'm doing a good job or not?' Once you answer that question, I'd like you to design a way to measure and report the answer. I'm not looking for trivia here, like how many flies you swatted this morning—just real business results that mean something to another person—like a customer. Here are some samples that Mike brought for us. I think this will be foundational to self-management—it might even be a deal-breaker if we don't get it right. For now, we'll refer to them as Key Performance Indicators, KPIs. What do you think?"

"When do you want them?" asked Scott wearily.

"We need them for our next all-hands meeting," Todd replied, without a hint of apology. "That's three weeks away. Deborah, can I meet with you privately for a few minutes?"

Deborah met Todd in his office. Todd got right to the point. "I'm going to ask a favor of you, because I know I can count on you to come through. I'd like you to provide some leadership on the KPIs. You're a spreadsheet ace. Take the next two days off, work at home, and knock out a list of KPIs for yourself and your staff. I want to show Scott and the others that this stuff is straightforward and give them an example to follow. We might even have a friendly competition to see which group can finish drafting their KPIs first. After accounting is complete, of course."

"Works for me!" Deborah replied. "I'd be happy to spend a couple of days at home. Working, of course!"

"Thanks, Deborah," Todd said. "Let me see what you come up with as soon as possible. Really appreciate it."

This is the list Deborah prepared for herself:

Deborah Moore

Process	KPI
Manage Cash	Average Interest Cost/Day

	Average Interest Rate
	Average Cash Balance
Prepare Financial Statements	Close Within One Day of End of Month
	Meet All Loan Covenants
Manage Risk	Average Insurance Cost/$100 Assets
	Loss Ratio
	Experience Modification Rate
Manage Financial Audit	Semiannual Audit Expense
Prepare Regulatory Filings	% Filings on Time

This was a graph she prepared for semiannual audit expense:

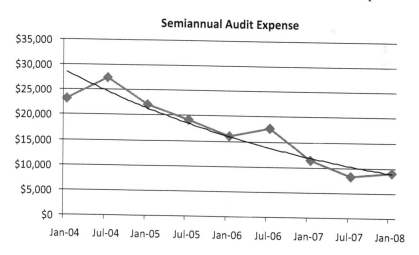

When she showed her work to Todd the following Monday, she was beaming. "You know, I realized the audit expenses were trending down, but didn't appreciate the magnitude until I could visualize it. I'm really happy with the way we've gotten things under control! Our team came up with more ideas for even greater savings—and turned it into a game. It's been fun."

Todd looked at the measures for the rest of her team, and expressed his appreciation for the thought that went into them. "I'd like to use these as examples for the rest of our leadership team," he said. "This is a great start. Thanks a lot for getting the ball rolling. Work should be a fun game—and fun is one of our top colleague-identified core values, after all.

"There's another component I'd like to address head on," he said. "You've done a great job identifying your processes, and associating your KPIs. Looks like there's a many-to-one relationship there—you can have multiple KPIs for any given process, which is great. But I'm concerned that not everyone has identified his or her processes as well as you have. And with all the hand-offs we have around here, that concerns me. Remember the brouhaha last month between sales and distribution over whether a product should have been designated for Synergy or a different customer? It seems like everyone was washing their hands of the problem and blaming the other department. I'd like to see that kind of behavior disappear. I think we need to rigorously identify our processes in order to support these Colleague Accountability Agreements and Key Performance Indicators. Here's a memo I prepared over the weekend. Take a look at it and tell me what you think. I'm open to suggestions for change."

Todd handed her his memo, which she took thoughtfully. "I'll take a look at it right away," she said. "It looks like it will take a pretty full repertoire of tools to make self-management work."

"I think that's right, Deborah," Todd replied. "And I've got a responsibility to make sure that all the pages are in the songbook. We have a big 'concert' coming up and we all have to sing in harmony."

Returning to his desk, Todd had some more thinking to do. He recognized the importance to self-management of well-executed and rigorous business processes delivering consistent value to customers. He hoped that his colleagues would see it the same way.

ᕗᕋ

This is the memorandum Todd wrote for his BerryWay colleagues:

To: All BerryWay Colleagues
From: Todd Brookstone
Date: April 20, 2008
Re: Business Process Management and Self-Management

Processes are sequences of activities that result in the creation of value for a customer, either internal or external. Core processes consist of those processes that result in the creation of value to the ultimate customer—in the case of BerryWay, the ultimate customer is the company that buys our products–without which we would not exist. Processes also include supporting processes (e.g. payroll), which are important but not the reason for being in business, and enabling processes (e.g. building permit acquisition), which allow the business to move forward but do not directly create value for customers. The very essence of our work is process execution and process innovation.

Processes are a big part of why we want to self-manage. Who knows more about a process than the person responsible for it? How could a manager possibly know as much about a process as the person executing it—much less make better real-time decisions about that process?

Solid business processes are valuable enterprise assets: they can be a source of differentiation and strategic advantage (think cross-docking logistics at Wal-Mart, or flexible production lines at Toyota). Poorly thought out or executed processes can, on the other hand, be non-advantageous or even liabilities. The best companies pay attention to their processes and have a process in place to continually improve them. They build a process mindset into the culture to take advantage of the knowledge base of their colleagues who are, after all, in the best position to identify and make improvements.

As BerryWay moves forward with development of Colleague Accountability Agreements (CAAs) and Key Performance Indicator (KPI) accountability, it becomes even more critical to define and refine its processes. Processes are the foundation for CAA and KPI accountability: they define the hand-offs and business rules for internal and external customers and suppliers. CAAs and KPIs define the accountability of individuals to each other and to the mission—but accountability for what? The process map supplies the what: every colleague becomes a steward for specific processes or activities within a process, with customers and suppliers to whom he or she is accountable.

We therefore need well-defined process maps to insure full individual and enterprise accountability—every process activity and related business decision must be assigned to an individual. This assignment defines, in turn, the process activities of an individual CAA to which one or more KPIs will be attached. And the customers and suppliers of an individual's processes will become the CAA colleagues of that colleague. The business risk of establishing CAAs without also examining processes is that there may be activities that are tacit, implied, or unexpressed but which are nonetheless real and important; and which therefore don't end up hitting anyone's CAA. And when the process breaks down, no one is responsible.

To be effective, we must define all BerryWay processes in detail and create a process mindset.

Embedding a process mindset in our culture will produce several key benefits:

- The enterprise has some 50 year-round and 200+ seasonal colleagues. No one knows more about how their area of the business works than these individuals. Harnessing their combined, collaborative mind power toward the goal of improving the business can and should reap substantial productivity gains.

- Day to day execution of processes will benefit from the stewardship of individuals who understand their processes intimately and watch the Key Performance Indicators to monitor process health.
- An enterprise with a process mindset will always have a strategic competitive advantage over an organization that doesn't—because a process culture leads to continuous improvement.
- A process mindset encourages innovation and initiative—since colleagues train themselves to think of ways to improve their processes—and hold each other accountable to do the same.
- A process mindset thinks beyond individual quirks, personalities and conflicts. A process culture values its processes as strategic assets, and seeks independence from individual knowledge bases and 'turf'.
- A process mindset is less political than a traditional corporate mindset and more willing to embrace disruptive change and growth.
- A process mindset encourages collaboration, especially between functional areas, breaking down barriers and information silos in pursuit of the common mission.
- It is axiomatic that if all enterprise processes are exposed to colleague analysis and improvement, the opportunities for improvement will increase. Breakdowns will trigger assistance from colleagues, motivated by the need to keep work flowing to or from other well-tuned processes. We therefore harness the existing power of peer collaboration.

The best processes are ones that take advantage of the collective intelligence of those charged with executing them. I'd like some ideas on how to build a process mindset within the BerryWay culture.

I respectfully request that you provide me with your ideas, questions, concerns, thoughts or suggestions for defining,

documenting and improving business processes by May 1.
Thank you.

The following day, with a couple of tweaks, Todd sent out
his memorandum to all colleagues, and called a meeting of his
leadership team.

"Have enough to work on so far?" Todd asked with a smile.

"Yes, I think so," Scott replied. "I'm trying to figure out how
to get any work done around here with all these initiatives."

"I appreciate that, Scott," Todd responded sympathetically.
"And I'm sure it's no consolation that self-management initiatives are consuming most of my time these days. But there are
just a few more pieces of the puzzle to set up before the next
all-hands meeting. So if you'll bear with me for just a few more
weeks, we'll get to where we need to be."

With that, Todd handed out the draft Colleague Accountability Agreement. "Our attorney, Heather Kay, worked with
us to come up with this agreement," he said. "I'd like you to
look at it and give me your feedback. What I'm proposing is
that all colleagues enter into this agreement with the people
they interface the most with—their closest work colleagues—
and commit to providing great service to them and to BerryWay
as an enterprise. People tend to take agreements seriously. I
wouldn't expect anyone to sign this without sincerely accepting
the responsibility it entails. If you have any recommendations,
please get them to me by tomorrow so we can move forward on
this."

"Also, as you know, I sent out my process memorandum today, and I'm also looking for feedback on it. All of these initiatives are linked, as you may have guessed. Defined processes
become elements of the Colleague Accountability Agreement,
along with their associated KPIs. No way to manage yourself
without tracking your results. Remember the old phrase 'what
gets measured gets done'? That's what we're about here today—
tying it all together. We have workgroups working on the mission, vision and principles—also part of the Colleague Account-

ability Agreement. And each colleague's representations on this agreement should align pretty squarely with their job description, competency model and results expectations—which in turn should provide a pretty solid springboard for each person's individual mission. I'm seeing lots of upside for self-management, but people will need tools to make it work. It's up to us as leaders to provide the tools.

"By the way," Todd continued. "We had some pretty great ideas on preferred culture the other day in our all-hands meeting. I'm proposing to add one more item to the list. I'd like to consciously build a process mindset into the culture. We should all be thinking about how work gets done, and how to get it done better, all the time. I'll take the liberty of adding it to the list, if that's okay with all of you.

"Just a couple more items before we break up. I've been thinking and talking to my network about this for a while now. Teresa, what do we do for orientation for new colleagues right now?" Todd asked.

"Give them the basics," Teresa replied. "I sit down with them and explain the work rules and benefits package, and answer any questions. They receive a packet of information. We take a plant tour, I introduce them to their immediate work colleagues, and we watch safety videos. We give them a password to the network and show them how the phones work. That's about it."

"And I do appreciate that process, Teresa," Todd responded. "But I'd like to do a bit more. Actually, we need to do quite a bit more. I'd like to establish a corporate university. I want a full three days of orientation for all new colleagues. I want them to be steeped in the industry, in the company culture, in their work processes, in everything. I want to provide training in effective communication. And I especially want to drive home the concept of self-management. We affect the culture every time a new person comes aboard. They bring with them their beliefs, their values, their strengths, and sometimes their baggage. It's not fair to them to throw them into an ecosystem where they're expected to self-manage without giving them all the tools and training they need to have a fighting chance at success. That's what we need to provide. Can we brainstorm right now and figure out what we need to provide in terms of core orientation training?"

This is what the team came up with:

BerryWay History and Culture
What is Self-Management?
Self-Management Tools and Techniques
Mission, Vision and Principles

"Can we brainstorm any courses that might enhance the success of self-management after orientation?" Todd asked the group. This is the list they created:

How to Take Initiative
Conflict Resolution
Effective Communication
Leadership
Negotiation Skills
Collaboration

Looking at the list, Todd turned to the group and asked a thought-provoking question. "Can anyone spot the themes here?"

"I see a theme of being proactive," Maria observed. "Moving forward, making progress, not succumbing to inertia. Taking initiative, resolving conflict suggests forward momentum to me."

"I agree with Maria, and would add effective interaction," said Teresa. "That's where I see the collaboration, communication and negotiation."

"Well, that leaves leadership. Where does that fit in?" asked Todd. "Is there even a role for leadership in an ecosystem of self-management?"

"I don't see where there's any room for leadership anymore," Scott observed. "It seems like in self-management, people will just go their own way and do their own thing. If I want to provide leadership, no one has to listen to me. Don't know why we'd even spend time thinking about it."

Todd suppressed his feeling of disappointment in Scott's viewpoint, and pressed on. "I think leadership is needed more than ever in a self-managed company," he said. "Leadership is what drives progress. Why would we need leadership any less in self-management than in hierarchy?" he asked rhetorically, to no one in particular.

"Leadership in a self-managed environment is different, however. The source is definitely not position, title or heredity. The only indication of a leader is whether someone has followers or not. In a self-managed environment, leadership is earned, not granted. Generally speaking, the person earning a position of leadership is the person with the most expertise to bring to bear on a particular problem or situation. And positions of leadership in self-managed situations aren't permanent. They revolve, depending on who has the most ability to deal with a situation, and whether people trust that person enough to follow him or her. I think leadership is absolutely vital in self-management. It's just that it's dynamic, not structured. A self-managed team may not even be able to identify who their leader is on any given day—and that's fine as long as they're learning from each other and making good things happen. And by the way, I'd be willing to pay good money to help our people become excellent leaders."

Scott sat, stony-faced, not responding.

"And if groups of people organically self-organize without apparent leadership around a problem or a process, that suits me just fine," Todd continued.

"I'm sure there are many courses we could add to a course catalog, but we don't have time to do that today," Todd observed, looking at his watch. "I do see the same themes that you do, however. If I had to boil it down, I'd call it 'leadership through proactive, effective interaction'. That could almost be the motto of our corporate university—and how we should think of ourselves as BerryWay colleagues. Teresa, would you be willing to drive that initiative? You won't have to resource the delivery of courses—yet. Just figure out the content, and we'll acquire the resources to deliver it. I think it's that important."

Teresa's face lit up at the challenge. "Can't wait to get started!" she responded. "It will be fun—just like being back in my corporate trainer days."

"Okay," said Todd. "A few more items. Teresa, I know your plate is rather full at the moment. But you heard me talk about implementing a full coaching and mentoring culture here at BerryWay. I don't want any colleague here to be 'stuck' without guidance of some sort. And we definitely want people to grow as professionals. I'd like you to design a mentoring program for all new colleagues and anyone else who wants to participate. I know W.L. Gore has a program they call 'sponsorship', for example. Perhaps you can benchmark what different companies do and then come back to us with a proposal. Again, I'm willing to finance any reasonable proposal—self-management is just that important to me. And I'd like you to line up a roster of business coaches who can assist any and all of our colleagues who are interested. Let me know what you come up with when you're ready. I won't hold you to having anything before the all-hands meeting next week."

Teresa nodded, pleased with Todd's display of confidence in her.

"There's another item for this leadership team to be aware of," Todd said. "Part of the Colleague Accountability Agreement has to do with decision rights. Hard to believe, I know, but not everyone gets to make the decision to build a new factory just because we've adopted a system of self-management. I'm not interested in a metaphysical discussion of where decision rights come from—not having time for metaphysics these days—but I do know that decisions need to be made in the business in order to serve our customers and other stakeholders, and colleagues should be crystal-clear on what decision authority they and other colleagues possess. So I'm proposing to link all business decisions to a process, which by definition will land on someone's Colleague Accountability Agreement, and then negotiating the scope of each person's decision-making authority with them and their process colleagues as part of the agreement.

"How should decision rights be allocated? Conceptually, it should be pretty straightforward. The person with the greatest expertise to bring to bear on a decision should be the person making the decision. Should that person collaborate with fellow colleagues, who may have pertinent information? Absolutely! But we need the best decision-makers for each decision to be in charge of that decision. Remember, in a system of voluntary association, like a newly self-managed company, everything is negotiable except the mission.

"We therefore have some major work to do," Todd continued. "We have to have an inventory of all processes for all areas of the company, and make sure that one or more colleagues own every process in their respective Colleague Accountability Agreements. Then we have to make sure we have Key Performance Indicators—at least a few—for each process. And we need to have decision rights assigned to each process that requires a decision. I would suggest that we're looking at a rather rigorous effort over the coming months.

"Final topic, I promise," Todd went on to say. "I think that people need to understand the competing demands of business. I'd like each area to have its own profit and loss statement and balance sheet. The concept is one of **business units**. The numbers will have to reflect some sort of transfer cost from one part of the process to the other, since we won't really have sales of product taking place from say, the filling machines to the warehouse. But we need to come up with a scheme that allows colleagues to think like businesspeople every hour of the day: how will expenses be affected by my decisions? What improvements can be made? How can I get more production out of these assets?

"I know that I can count on you, Deborah, to come up with a reporting system that can facilitate this. I'd like each area to play with strategy, for example. There's no reason all strategy in the organization has to come from me. There will be some quirky areas to address, like R&D and administration, which will probably have to be treated like service companies. But I'm confident we can get it done through hard work. Each one of our electro-mechanic colleagues is already personally responsible for millions of dollars in equipment. I can't operate or repair it, and neither can you, Scott. They're in charge of more assets than most small-company CEOs. We need to start treating them that way. I want a company of professional businesspeople. That's my dream. I can't wait for the hands-on meeting next week to start the countdown to self-management."

While most of his leadership team nodded affirmatively, Scott looked skeptical. "Here's the money question, and I'll bet you don't have an answer," said Scott with a slight smirk. "You say you want self-management. But throughout the history of this company, you've determined all salaries, wage rates, benefits and pay increases. That means you've got all the power. So even if you come up with a system and label it 'self-management', you still have the power. So it's really just the same thing, dressed up to look like something else."

"Okay, Scott, fair enough if I wanted to retain all decision rights to compensation. But I don't. I want everyone to set their own salary, within certain common-sense guidelines of competitive salary levels." The meeting became very quiet. Scott looked puzzled.

"You see, most people want to do the right thing. As the legal owner, I have primary stewardship of decisions involving large sums of money, like payroll. My name is on all the personal guarantees, for example. Would anyone here like to assume personal responsibility for, say, $250 million dollars of debt? I wouldn't expect you'd want to. So I have certain positive obligations to steward the finances of the enterprise. And it's true that, up until now, I have personally signed off on all pay decisions, leaning heavily on Teresa's analysis, of course.

"But I'm happy to have those days come to an end, under self-management. Teresa will publish the salary ranges for your skills, abilities and positions, and you can pick any number from that range. It's totally up to you. You and all your colleagues will pick your own salary. No one will pick, say, $1 million per year, because our financial assets couldn't support it. Perhaps we can even include a reasonable band above the market range to allow for colleagues who are contributing more to the enterprise than most. But here's the kicker, the responsibility counterweight to responsible free choice: you *will* be expected to perform to whatever salary level you select. If you pick high, the expectations will be high. And if you meet those expectations, everyone wins. But if you pick a high salary and don't meet expectations, you can expect to renegotiate that salary with me the following year. And we will have very good data in front of us for that discussion.

"I would love nothing better than to pay very high salaries for very high performance, and share the fruits of that performance with you and all our colleagues. I expect more from people in a self-managed environment. I expect fewer problems, especially people problems, to hit my desk—because I'm counting on a group of highly professional self-managers to deal with the stuff that managers in traditional companies are paid to deal with. I'd also be very interested in tying variable pay to business unit performance as we move forward.

"Here's the corollary, however: if anyone wants to renegotiate their salary level at any time, that's not a problem. You will need to present a business case, however, for the increase—more than the fact that you're already doing your normal job. And that holds true for any annual increase beyond the cost of living—you must make a business case demonstrating your demonstrable ongoing and future increased value to the organization.

"So Scott, after we formally adopt self-management in the near future, come see me and tell me how much you want to be paid." With that, Todd adjourned the meeting. He was exhausted, and felt a slight twinge in his left side. He made a mental note to visit the doctor in the near future.

∽

Todd met the next morning with the workgroup volunteers from the last all-hands meeting. The volunteers elected Shannon Young, a bright and upcoming marketing intern, to deliver their findings. Here is what she enthusiastically presented:

Mission
Our Mission is to create memorable Willamette Valley-sourced food experiences through Value, Quality and Service.

Our Values and Principles
1. We, the colleagues of BerryWay, hereby commit to work together for the mission in a spirit of teamwork, helping each other in a harmonious way to achieve great things.
2. We agree as individuals to exercise initiative to take any and all necessary actions required to achieve the mission.
3. We agree to communicate, coordinate and collaborate with each other as professional colleagues in a spirit of productive fun and dedication.
4. We agree to earn the trust of one another by keeping commitments and promises, by communicating, and by pursuing professional competence at the highest possible level of sustained performance.
5. We agree to ethically conduct ourselves with honesty and integrity at all times.
6. We agree to hold each other accountable for business results and adhering to the mission and values and principles, using tact and clarity.
7. We agree to tolerate each other's differences, and to care about one another as individuals and colleagues.
8. We agree to engage in business practices that are transparent and open.

9. We agree to pursue innovative solutions to problems and to pursue innovative opportunities for improvement.
10. We agree to pursue lofty performance through superior efficiency and effectiveness.
11. We agree to structure our agreements in a way that allows all parties to benefit.
12. We agree to pursue our mission and objectives with enthusiasm and vigor.
13. We agree to support and uphold flexibility in the methods used to achieve our objectives and those of our colleagues.
14. We agree to the following method for Resolving Conflict, and to seek opportunity in conflict for improved relationships.
    A. Colleagues shall discuss issues relating to activities not supportive of the mission or not honoring of these values and principles, or any work-related issue, directly with other colleagues.
    B. If colleagues are unable to resolve issues directly, then they agree to discuss the issue with a trusted third party.
    C. If still unable to resolve the issue, colleagues agree to discuss the issue with a quorum of three colleagues, whereupon the facts will be heard and a decision made in light of the facts and the mission.
    D. Colleagues agree to pursue and support a quick resolution.

Todd listened carefully, taking notes. When Shannon concluded her presentation, Todd thanked the team for their hard work, and smiled inwardly. He was proud of the workgroup, and optimistic about the future of self-management.

༄

The following morning would bring next all-hands meeting. The date was April 30, and the factory was busy gearing up for another season while swirling with conversation about the big changes Todd was introducing. Todd wanted and needed one last all-hands meeting to tie everything together, and to start a one-month countdown to self-management. He looked forward to briefing his advisory board. He arrived at Sean's office promptly at 4:00 p.m.

"I think we're prepared for the meeting," Todd said to his trusted advisors. "We have a mission, values and principles with a conflict resolution process. We have a set of agreed-upon cultural imperatives to address. For supporting systems, we have a draft Colleague Accountability Agreement, containing an individual mission aligned with the company mission, Process Accountabilities, Key Performance Indicators and Decision Rights. In many cases, we can pull our excellent job descriptions directly across into the agreements with minor modifications. We have a strong new business process initiative in the works. We'll have a new corporate university with rigorous orientation training for all new colleagues, and a catalog of courses for ongoing professional development. We'll provide mentoring for all new colleagues and all colleagues who want it, as well as executive coaching for those who can benefit. We create freedom and space for natural leadership to develop and thrive in response to the needs of the enterprise. And we're launching business units to expose all colleagues to the rigors of P&L accountability. And people are going to set their own salaries. It's going to be quite a meeting.

"My idea is to tie everything together, and begin a one-month countdown to official adoption where we can continue meeting, answering questions, and begin working on the agreements," Todd continued. "Why don't all of you come to the meeting and see how I do?"

"Thanks for the invite, Todd," Sandra said. "I'll be there. Who else wants to go?" Sean and Bill both nodded in the affirmative.

"I wouldn't miss it for the world," Bill said. "And you'd better get a good night's sleep, Todd. I feel like I'm watching one of those Saturn V rockets building thrust on the launch pad, just waiting for the gantry to fall away so it can take off. You can count on us to help any way we can."

Todd went home, greeted Sarah, felt the baby move, then went to bed and fell asleep as soon as his head hit the pillow.

∽

Todd conducted the meeting the next morning with alacrity. He articulated the reasoning behind each initiative, answered all questions, and introduced his advisory team to his colleagues. He kicked off a process for colleagues to express questions and concerns regarding the various self-management initiatives that were under way over the next thirty days. With the assent of those in attendance, he started the countdown to official adoption of self-management. He saw a few looks of skepticism, but mostly felt appreciation if not total understanding from his colleagues. He was proud of them and their willingness to embrace change. To Todd's surprise, this had turned out to be the smoothest meeting so far.

At the end of the meeting, Todd turned to answer a question and felt a sharp pain in his left side. He finished answering his colleague, thanked his advisory board for attending, and quickly left the building for his car.

Chapter Six: Acid Test

୧⁓୨

Two weeks had elapsed since the commencement of the one-month countdown to self-management. Todd had just finished conducting his second forum for all those with questions and concerns, and left feeling very good about the session and the momentum toward self-management. He still worried about some of his colleagues, including Scott, and the possibility of a union campaign. He resolved to cross those bridges when he came to them. It was time for his doctor's appointment.

୧⁓୨

The doctor looked at Todd directly, the lab reports on the table beside him. "It's definitely cancer, Todd. We need to perform surgery tomorrow, and then figure out a game plan based on what we find."

Todd breathed out slowly, trying to keep his sudden rush of panic in check. Sarah looked stricken. He had to get through this; he had to move forward. He had felt impervious, he realized. No choices remained now. He would be out of action for a while—but he would be back. As he drove home with Sarah, he tried to convey his confidence and resolve: "I need to meet with my leadership team today and get some things organized. This is going to be a test for us, but I think we can handle it." He smiled reassuringly at his wife, who couldn't smile back.

Later that afternoon, he pulled slowly into the factory parking lot, wondering how the leadership team would react to his news. He had wanted them to take full advantage of the freedom of self-management. Now, he felt, they would have no choice but to self-manage. He wouldn't be available to them for a while.

He walked slowly and painfully into the conference room and eased himself into one of the big chairs. His leaders were already positioned around the table, looking at him eagerly for some sign of what he wanted to talk about. Rick, the new acquisition leader, who was still getting acclimated to the culture, joined them. Todd made a mental note to spend some quality time with Rick once he got healthy, to help get him up to speed. Finally, Todd broke the silence.

"I'm sick," he said simply. "Cancer. I'm having surgery tomorrow, and likely followed by a regimen of chemotherapy and possibly radiation." He paused to let his words sink in.

"As you may know, Sean is my trustee and will assume the duties of president if anything happens to me. He will step into my shoes and have all legal responsibility and authority for BerryWay. Since most of you know Sean, I'm confident that such an arrangement will work fine if it becomes necessary." The leaders around the table looked at Todd with various mixtures of sympathy, shock and sadness.

Deborah broke the silence. "We're coming up on the launch of self-management in just two weeks," she said. "Do you think we should hold off?"

Todd fixed her with a big smile. "Absolutely not!" he said. "If anything, this will be the acid test. If a company can continue to function, without its ostensible leader, it can't help but strengthen and validate self-management. Of course we should continue. Why don't you give me an update on how our initiatives are progressing?"

Each person took a turn briefing Todd on that status of the various self-management initiatives. All were progressing according to schedule, further convincing Todd that delay was unnecessary. BerryWay should be a self-managed company in fourteen days, whether Todd was there or not. He was pleased with the progress of his colleagues.

Todd addressed his team for the last time before surgery. "I'd like you to work with each other to conduct the remaining meetings and continue to drive the various self-management initiatives. Deborah, please make sure that everyone understands the Colleague Accountability Agreement and gets their questions answered. As much as possible, try to keep up with the schedule that I had planned. I'll return to work as soon as I can." He stood up awkwardly and left with a painful wave and forced smile. It would be a different company when he returned.

&

On June 1, the colleagues of BerryWay met with Sean Baker and the rest of Todd's advisory team. There were briefings from colleagues on the status of all the self-management initiatives, including the Colleague Accountability Agreements, the Key Performance Indicators, the business process initiative, and all other aspects. With the sole exception of Scott, Todd's leadership team had stepped up and done a beautiful job coordinating with each other to drive Todd's vision to the point of adoption. All that remained was to have the colleagues adopt a formal declaration of self-management, drafted earlier by Todd.

"Well, I understand you've had a lot of meetings and done a lot of work," Sean opened the meeting. "And you've had a chance to read Todd's simple declaration of self-management. What would you like to do?"

David raised his hand. "I'd like to propose that we adopt self-management as a way of life at BerryWay, as of today, using the systems and tools that we've been developing," he said. "There is no way that anyone who works here can say they haven't had a chance to express themselves on this issue. If anyone here doesn't know what self-management is all about by now, they probably never will. It's time to declare."

"Any other comments? Objections? Questions?" Sean asked one final time. "Hearing none, we can all assume that we're ready to move forward. I'll pass this declaration around for you to sign, and report the news to Todd, and I know he'll appreciate hearing it. Thank you for your time, and good luck!" He knew from conversations with Todd and Deborah that virtually all the spadework had already been done, and the declaration was most-ly a formality. Still, it represented a symbolic break with the past, and would be meaningful to those who participated. He also found it interesting that Scott, the production leader, was miss-ing from the meeting. He made a note to mention that to Todd.

༄

Todd looked at the tube in his arm, feeding him the tox-ic chemicals he needed to fight his disease. The surgery had gone well, and all visible traces of cancer had been removed. He would have to endure six months of chemotherapy, but avoided the need for radiation, for which he was grateful. Sean entered the room with a big smile.

"Well, I guess you've got a self-managed company," he said. "Congratulations!"

"Thanks, Sean. I appreciate you taking care of that last piece of business for me. They said I could go back to work in two weeks, and I can't wait. I'm going stir-crazy here," Todd replied.

"I think your leadership team is doing an outstanding job, Todd," Sean continued. "I have one concern, though. Scott Thorsen wasn't at the final meeting. What's his angle?"

"That's somewhat surprising and yet, somewhat not sur-prising," Todd observed. "Of all the leaders in the company, he's been the one throwing up the most roadblocks to self-management. I think it's fair to expect a little resistance, given his background in traditional organizations, but I would have expected him to be there unless there were some kind of emer-gency." Todd made a note on a sheet of paper to investigate Scott's level of commitment when he got back to work.

༄

When Todd returned, the colleagues greeted him in the caf-eteria with a cake and balloons. Sitting down to a large piece of chocolate cake, he accepted the good wishes of his colleagues, and shared some jokes and teasing about his unusually slight appearance. Despite feeling somewhat tired, he was glad to be back and eager to learn how things were progressing.

Later, in his office, Maria greeted him with a hug. "So glad you're back!" she exclaimed. "We missed you! But we want you to know that we kept things running well in your absence.

"There is one thing you need to know about," she said, turning suddenly serious. "The concern over a possible union campaign appears to have been justified. Right after the declaration of self-management on June 1, Jill and another lab technician, Andrew, both quit. There were several unsigned union cards in her vacated desk. My guess is that any card-check campaign never got traction, because you were so passionate in selling us on the benefits of self–management. At any rate, we've never been notified about needing an election. It looks like freedom wins."

Todd thanked Maria for the news, and resolved that he would have to meet with Scott, and soon. He couldn't afford to have such an influential colleague disengaged.

☙

Deborah approached Todd's office with a look of urgency. "Looks like we get a chance to test our conflict resolution process," she said. "We need you to serve as a mediator in a conflict resolution."

"What's up?" Todd asked with curiosity. He hadn't heard anything about a conflict until now.

"The grapevine was swirling with stories about Scott threatening to replace one of his equipment suppliers for missing a deadline," she said. "I decided to confront Scott about it, because I see all the purchase orders, and I knew that the so-called deadline was non-existent. He had revised the P.O. to ensure the supplier couldn't meet the new terms, and ordered the same kind of equipment from a different supplier at a higher price—one that happens to be taking him on a fishing trip to Alaska next week. And you know what? Scott admitted the behavior! I couldn't believe it—so alien to the culture we're trying to create around here. I was furious that he was undermining all of our hard work at BerryWay. And I asked him to exit the company."

Todd looked at his trusted associate with admiration for her fierce defense of the company. "You're right. I guess we'll find out how well self-management works now," he said finally.

∽

Deborah and Scott sat on opposite sides of the conference table, not looking at one another. Todd entered the room and closed the door. "Where are we?" said Todd, taking a chair at the head of the table.

"Well, we're at step two," Deborah said. "I've made a request, Scott has declined. Now we'd like you to mediate our dispute. It would appear that we're at an impasse."

"What do you have to say, Scott?" Todd asked politely. "Apparently, you haven't been able to persuade your colleague, Deborah, of the soundness of your position so far. What can you tell me that will change things?"

"I'm a self-managed professional," Scott answered. "I own the decision to purchase equipment for the production area. That means I have the choice of where to purchase it."

"I see," Todd replied. "Let's review the facts. Deborah says you revised a purchase order to add a delivery deadline that wasn't part of your original agreement with the supplier. Is that right?" Scott's silence answered for him.

"I see further that you actually paid a higher price for the same piece of equipment by buying it from a different manufacturer—true?" Todd continued relentlessly. Scott looked down at the floor.

"And finally, I'm told that this second manufacturer is taking you on an expense-paid Alaskan fishing trip next week—true?" Todd bore in with the careful precision of a surgeon's scalpel. Scott had nothing to say.

"Here's how I see it, Scott," Todd pressed forward, wanting his points to be crystal clear. "Let's look at the mission. We are creating memorable Willamette Valley-sourced food experiences through value, quality and service. Guess I'm not quite sure how overpaying for equipment provides value. Could you enlighten me?

"And I also like Paragraph Five of our Values and Principles: 'We agree to conduct ourselves with ethics, honesty and integrity at all times'," Todd continued. "Not real sure how changing a contract retroactively to make it one-sided has much to do with ethics, honesty and integrity. And that reminds me of Paragraph Eleven: 'We agree to structure our agreements in a way that allows all parties to benefit.' Doesn't look like the original supplier enjoyed much benefit, does it? Do we really need to explore the fishing trip as well?"

"Well, according to our self-management principles, you don't have the unilateral authority to fire me," Scott said finally.

"Right you are, Scott!" Todd replied. "But think about it. Do you really want to admit this behavior to a quorum of colleagues? It's pretty clear to me that what you're engaged in here is wrong, and I personally would prefer not to associate with you professionally after this."

"Fine. I'll find somewhere else to work," Scott said. "But what makes you so smart, anyway, that you can uproot a company's culture and totally change the way we do business?"

Todd leaned forward slowly and brought both arms in front of him on the table, and fixed his now-former colleague with eyes of cold blue steel. "You're absolutely right. I'm not that smart, Scott. Really. I'm just a guardian of the mission."

Following the exchange with Scott, one of Berryway's product development scientists, Megan, asked Todd to mediate a difference of opinion with another scientist regarding which product choices to test market in the coming fiscal year. The two technical colleagues had maintained a respect for each other's expertise, but had come to differing conclusions about quality and product performance data and were at an impasse. Todd was happy to help grapple with a problem that seemed amenable to rigorous questioning and statistical analysis. After spending three solid hours with the two colleagues, the three had arrived at a happy medium backed by solid quantitative support. They would fully back Megan's proposed product mix for the coming year, and alternate with her colleague's proposal in the year following.

Todd noted to himself that even though the latest mediation took much longer than the intense discussion with Scott, he felt invigorated and energized. He was having fun again. Even more interesting, he felt that his company had arrived at a product testing decision that was of the highest quality. Even though Megan and her colleague had taken weeks to prepare and discuss their proposals, all the data had been beautifully summarized to support the best possible overall decision. Todd reflected that he was merely the catalyst needed to bring the two scientists into a final accord. They had all the power within themselves all along to take the right course of action. He felt proud of them, and happy with the result.

Flicking off the lights to leave, Todd made a mental note to meet with Teresa the next day. They needed to incorporate the concept of self-management into every people process: recruitment, selection, orientation, feedback, coaching and compensation—and to infuse their competency models with self-management skills. The new culture would obviate the need to manage others—as long as their processes supported and strengthened it. Todd realized that nurturing their culture was now his most important role.

Stepping into the late afternoon sun, Todd smiled inwardly. He was excited to see how high their fledgling company could fly on its newly-unfurled, gossamer wings of freedom.

Chapter Seven: Epilogue

Todd looked out his picture window across the Santiam River at the moonlit forest, sipping a coffee. He reflected that BerryWay had grown to three times its original size in the last few years, and supplied an expanding market that was starting to push overseas. Todd noted with satisfaction that the company's growth curve had turned sharply upward after the adoption of self-management, accompanied by solid profitability. There had been many challenges along the way, and much learning. His outlook on life had changed as a result of his illness. Every moment was more priceless. He and Sarah had welcomed a son the year before, and Todd thought about the joys of fatherhood, of being a husband and the gift of dedicated colleagues and friends.

He looked at his young family, playing on the large brown rug in front of the fireplace. Freedom is a wonderful thing, he thought. In the workplace, no less than anywhere else, freedom works. He rose, kissed his wife and son, and went to bed.

Chapter Eight: Self-Management Comes to the Organization

⌘

W.L. Gore & Associates

There is a reason that W.L. Gore consistently ranks in the top tier of *Fortune* magazine's annual list of "100 Best Companies to Work For": people love to work in an innovative, self-organizing environment. As Alan Deutschman wrote in *Fast Company* in 2004: "Pound for pound, the most innovative company in America is W.L. Gore & Associates."[2] Gore's spirit of innovation extends well beyond Gore products into the existential core of its organizational ecosystem. It implicitly embraces the essence of self-management through its emphasis on teamwork, natural leadership, relative freedom and individual initiative.

Former Gore executive Joyce Bowlsbey met a colleague and I at the W.L. Gore Elk Mills fabric plant in the lush, rolling green hills of the Maryland countryside just west of Newark, Delaware, on a rainy June morning. A manufacturer of high-performance outdoor apparel, Glide dental floss (sold to Procter and Gamble in 2003), Elixir guitar strings, and industrial and insulation materials, Gore became famous in Tom Peter's best-selling business books for its renowned "lattice" organizational structure.

Joyce had been a Gore associate (*all* Gore employees are known as associates) for eighteen years. She was the lead internal sales associate for the fabric division, probably the best known of all of the Gore divisions. Her husband had been with Gore for 33-years; he was the 64th associate hired by Bill Gore in

2 Alan Deutschman, *The Fabric of Creativity, http://www.fastcompany. com/magazine/89/open_gore.html*, December 1, 2004.

the early days of the company. A savvy and articulate representative for the company, Joyce was very open about the famed lattice structure.

Joyce had been a public face for Gore, involved in public speaking and active in her community; and well versed in all aspects of the Gore culture and organizational philosophy. She continued to work at Gore because she loved her job and believed in the Gore ideals and philosophy. She was extraordinarily gracious, generous with her time, and patient with our questions.

The Elk Mills #5 plant, a 250,000 square-foot facility, was only one month old at the time of our visit. A beautiful building and sparkling clean, it had not yet ramped up to full capacity. A handful of associates staffed the entire facility. We visited most parts of the factory, including the R&D laboratory, production floor and distribution area.

The factory would eventually employ about 200 associates per shift on two shifts per day, a technical departure from the original Gore philosophy of employing only 200 associates *per factory* to maintain familiarity among associates. It was apparent that simple production economics drove the decision to enlarge the size of this newest factory, which would make large quantities of garments for resellers like Columbia Sportswear and Northface. Other significant Gore customers included the Department of Defense, NASA and various police agencies worldwide.

In Gore's climate labs, local college students would soon subject themselves to wild variations in temperature and humidity to test extreme-wear clothing. In a two-story "rain-room", garments–sometimes worn by volunteers—would be exposed to varying pressures of artificial rain to test waterproofing. Quality was assured in a large lab where machines and human researchers stretched, pulled, tore and repeatedly washed raw and finished fabric.

Gore was justifiably proud of its heritage, highlighted by a large display case containing its most famous garments, including the cold-weather suit worn by explorer Will Steger on his Arctic expeditions, flight suits, ocean sailing suits, football jerseys, and other fascinating examples of "extreme-wear". Gore also placed a premium on first impressions for visitors. The comfortable and spacious reception area and well-stocked cafeteria were warm and friendly, staffed by gracious and friendly associates who made us feel welcome from the moment of our arrival.

The production area and inventory storage and shipping areas were, in a word, huge. These areas comprised the bulk of the giant facility. Large fabric storage racks, partially filled with large rolls of various fabrics, dotted the facility. Giant automated looms, expertly operated by a single associate, hummed in the background. The basic process involved converting raw fabric into Gore-Tex water-resistant material to make parkas, pants, boots, socks and other garments. The cavernous empty spaces would soon be filled with raw and finished inventory in the run-up to full production. The production processes appeared to be fairly standardized to limit variability and error. Line balancing seemed to be the primary production challenge. Gore cross-trained associates and taught them to assist with production bottlenecks if necessary to maintain smooth line flow.

Freestanding modular offices occupied another part of the facility. The office spaces were organized by function: administrative personnel were grouped together, as were sales associates. There were temporary office spaces set aside for visiting associates needing a workspace with a desk, phone, and computer link. Scattered throughout the office area were mini-conference rooms, with tables, easels and phones for meetings to accommodate two to seven people. There were even smaller equally equipped meeting rooms for use by one to three people. It was in one of these smaller rooms that we met with Joyce to discuss Gore's organizational philosophy following our tour. The only traditional offices we observed belonged to human resource associates (for privacy reasons) and for quality assurance researchers near the laboratories. The large main office was clearly designed to promote interactive communication and information sharing.

Joyce described the overall corporate culture as being in transition. Bill Gore, the entrepreneurial dynamo who created

W.L. Gore and Associates with his wife and partner Genevieve ("Vieve" to Gore associates) in the basement of their Newark, Delaware home in 1958, had passed away several years earlier. His son, Bob Gore, was the president at the time of our visit. The company was in the process of identifying non-family members within the organization who could provide the energy, vision and strategy to take the company into the next century.[3]

Joyce described the Gore Company she knew when she first came to work eighteen years earlier, when Bill Gore was still the driving entrepreneurial force in the company. Bill would spend countless hours in the factories talking to associates about every aspect of their jobs. His personality was competitive, driven, and hands-on. At that time, the company had a very familial and paternalistic feeling, where everyone worked and socialized together. Since Bill's death, the company outgrew its small family business atmosphere, becoming slightly more impersonal with less socializing (other then the annual company picnic and Christmas party). Another force detracting from the original open and fun atmosphere, according to Joyce, was the increase in employment-related litigation—problems obviously not unique to W.L. Gore. Joyce felt that more time would be needed in the future to orient new associates around the idea of commitment to the mission and principles.

Gore's basic organizational structure is flat. Anyone can discuss any issue with anyone else, up to and including the CEO. They describe this as a lattice organization—defined as a horizontal network of peers. Gore likes to emphasize that no one at Gore is anointed a leader. Leaders emerge naturally, defined by their followers.

Each Gore division has its own mission statement, and each individual associate creates their own personal commercial mission statement. The individual mission statements are ideally reviewed and revised annually. More important than mission statements, however, were Bill Gore's four key principles, which Joyce easily recited from memory:

3   Terri Kelly became President and CEO in 2005.

- Fairness to each other and everyone with whom we come in contact with;
- Freedom to encourage, help and allow other associates to grow in knowledge, skill, scope of responsibility;
- The ability to make one's own commitments and keep them;
- Consultation with other associates before undertaking actions that could negatively impact the company by hitting it "below the waterline."

To assist every associate at Gore to adhere to these key principles and help them fulfill their mission, each new associate is assigned a sponsor. The role of sponsor is not synonymous with hierarchical management or traditional supervision. Sponsors are generally selected because of their people skills—the ability to convey trust and confidence—and are people to whom others naturally gravitate for support and help. Generally, sponsors are responsible for about five associates at a time. To an associate, a sponsor is part coach, part mentor, part sounding board, part advocate and part Sherpa. Sponsors play a crucial role in bringing new associates on board and keeping them on track. They have the formal role of proactively tracking an associate's progress and *assisting* them as needed—but as an advisor, not a boss. The sponsor usually will give a new associate a verbal six-month evaluation and a written evaluation after twelve months. A twelve-month evaluation is given to all associates. Joyce felt that formal sponsorship was a powerful shaping force to promote Gore values and principles.

Every associate at Gore, whether new or incumbent, has a sponsor. When an associate comes to a sponsor with a problem (such as a conflict with a fellow associate) the sponsor is trained in role-playing potential scenarios to help the associate visualize and solve the problem herself. All associates are trained to use "I" messages with fellow associates: not "you always make me mad!" but rather "I feel upset when you do that". There are three types of sponsors: starting sponsors, contribution sponsors and compensation sponsors (more about these later). These roles may be divided among different sponsors or embodied in a single sponsor. Associates do have the right to request a new sponsor based on personality fit.

As in all human organizations, Gore has its share of personnel problems, ego trips and personality clashes. As the first ones to encounter these issues, sponsors carefully document and appropriately mentor associates. Every attempt is made to resolve a problem to avoid dismissing an associate. Gore strongly encourages and trains its people in effective interpersonal communication. For example, all associates undergo Leadership Effectiveness Training (LET) during orientation to learn problem solving and conflict resolution techniques. This training appears to be extraordinarily influential in teaching constructive solutions to problems before they escalate.

Apart from its unique organizational philosophy, Gore is widely known as one of the planet's most innovative companies—delivering amazing results to customers (after all, if the world didn't value Gore products, its organizational structure wouldn't matter very much). But it seems clear that Gore owes a large part of its reputation for innovation to its flexible lattice organization.

As evidence of the symbiosis between Gore's reputation for technical innovation and its self-managed organizational structure, associates in research and development have the freedom to form flexible teams around specific research projects. Researchers at Gore freely band together to study and research a particular innovation to a logical conclusion, then disband and form new teams based on new innovations.

One of the best innovation examples is the invention of Elixir guitar strings, summarized in an article by Gary Haber at DelawareOnline[4]:

Elixir, which debuted in 1997, sprang from the mind of a W.L. Gore employee in the company's medical products division,

---

4   Gary Haber, *W.L. Gore: Weathering 50 Years of Change*, http://www. delawareonline.com/article/20080106/NEWS/801060346/W-L-Gore-Weathering-50-years-of-change, January 6, 2008.

a musician who honed the idea during what the company calls "dabble time," the unscripted hours it gives employees to spend poking into projects that interest them.

Joyce beautifully summed up the Gore organizational philosophy with her own list of bullet points:

- No fixed or assigned authority
- Natural leadership defined by natural followership
- Objectives established by consensus
- Person-to-person communication encouraged
- Tasks and functions organized by commitments

W.L Gore & Associates is an obvious pioneer in espousing and successfully implementing concepts that have made it an icon of workplace freedom.

Nucor

At first blush, a steel company would not seem to be a natural candidate for organizational self-management: tightly defined, discrete functions must be highly focused and coordinated in a unified, well-managed process. The end product must be stored, sold and shipped as soon as possible at the highest possible price. Is there room for self-management?

On a sunny late September day, the friendly Vice President of Human Resources, Jim Coblin, greeted a colleague and I with a firm handshake at the modest and comfortable Charlotte, North Carolina headquarters of Nucor. We soon learned that Nucor knows the low end of the commodity steel market better than anyone. We learned that they really know how to build teams of committed, motivated and self-organizing people. And we learned that Nucor is a high-performance self-management engine with an ultra-thin coating of traditional structure.

Jim told us about the Nucor team concept, where Nucor forms teams around functions like casting, rolling, straightening, melting, and shipping. Team members start at relatively low base wages in the $8-$10 per hour range (unionized competitor U.S. Steel pays $18-$19 per hour).

Very high weekly performance bonuses drive performance. Nucor bases the weekly performance bonuses on productivity–Quality Tons of Steel Produced Per Week (by functional team). The bonuses—initially opposed by the finance department as too risky—are unrelated to profit. Jim explained that the Production Incentive Plan covers 80% of the Nucor workforce, and that bonuses can be 100% of the base wage, with no stipulated maximum. Nucor pays its maintenance personnel the average bonus of teams served during the week. Not surprisingly, everyone tracks the metric of Quality Tons of Steel Per Week. And Nucor expects its plant managers and other leaders to track a lot more than that.

Simplicity and brilliant clarity are the hallmarks of the Nucor production bonus plan. Every Nucor employee can explain the bonus program, can follow the production numbers as they update and predict their own bonus amounts. There are no politics in the system, since all bonuses are 100% non-discretionary and objective, based entirely on performance.

Production targets–set at about 80% of equipment capacity–remain constant, and are not raised by increasing throughput. A major goal is for everyone to engage with the bonus plan. A typical bonus is 5% of a worker's base wage for each ton of steel over 8 tons/hour, so long as product quality is acceptable. A worker straightening 30 tons per hour of steel on equipment designed to straighten 10 tons per hour, can receive $24 per hour during overtime, on an $8 per hour base wage (paid at time-and-a-half). Working overtime can really pay off, since overtime is paid on the bonus rate, not the base. Changes in the cost of living generally guide any annual base pay adjustments for production workers.

Nucor does have managers, although very few layers. The attitude of managers is that they are there to help the people performing the actual work—not to boss them around. And hourly workers are heartily encouraged to tell managers what resources they need to get the job done—and what obstacles to performance need to be removed.

Nucor nurtures its unique culture carefully, intentionally seeding new teams with experienced hands. Only when team members have fully absorbed the necessary knowledge and skill to perform at a high level is the team cut loose to do its job.

The culture has key attributes and tacit understandings that guide performance. There are very clear rules in the workplace: if you're tardy, you lose your bonus for the day. If you're absent, you lose your bonus for the week. As might be expected, the incidence of absenteeism and tardiness trends toward zero, giving Nucor a huge competitive advantage in its largely unionized industry. The clarity of the rules inhibits politics, which Nucor employees appreciate.

Nucor's excursion into the swirling rapids of self-management is guided by their invisible yet rigorous "unofficial justice system." Why have layers of management, when colleagues themselves police each other and maintain the performance culture? Peer accountability (or peer pressure), is a powerful influencing factor driving performance at Nucor. Jim noted that sometimes workers have literally chased lazy colleagues off the job site. And why not? To allow a Nucor colleague to slide is a direct personal financial hit. And Nucor allows no fill-ins: when someone is absent, the remaining team members pick up the slack. While Nucor colleagues often refer friends and relatives, they tend not to refer those who would slack off—costing bonus money. Factory employees, however, are not directly involved in the selection process.

Nucor must be doing something right. It enjoys a harmonious marriage of the lowest per-ton labor cost in the industry with the highest paid steel workforce in the world. Because the world appreciates what the company produces, Nucor has never needed to lay anyone off—a great economic benefit to the semi-rural areas where Nucor locates its mini-mills. And it doesn't hurt workforce loyalty to employ high school graduates who earn $75,000 to $80,000 per year, have the right to buy Nucor stock at a discount, and participate in a 401k.

While remaining non-union, due process prevails at Nucor. Employees are allowed to file grievances, and to appeal the outcomes. Nucor employees don't necessarily like the rotating shifts demanded by the exigencies of round-the-clock production. But the pay and benefits, coupled with the supportive culture, still make Nucor an attractive place to work.

Philosophically, Nucor doesn't treat its general administration and sales people differently from the workers on the factory floor—a significant cultural marker. A department manager might have base pay that is 20-25% below market, but receive an annual bonus based on return on assets for his or her particular factory, averaging 75% of the base. Other professionals receive a wage or salary relative to the overall labor market (it would be hard to find a secretary willing to work for 75% of the labor market rate), but can receive up to 30% of base pay relative to the return on assets for their plant. Headquarters personnel receive a bonus based on the ROA of all Nucor plants combined.

Like W.L. Gore & Associates, Nucor plants are basically stand-alone entities, each one led by a Plant Manager with VP/corporate officer status. Individual plants handle their own payroll, sales, purchasing, and legal affairs. The most mission-critical responsibilities include human resources management, energy procurement and raw material procurement. Executive pay, including pay for plant managers, is usually based on the return on shareholder equity for the entire corporation—encouraging collaboration and cross-fertilization of ideas among plants. Smart managers know when to ask for help—a key attribute of effective self-management. Managerial failure is usually traceable to a lack of interpersonal skills.

The old school culture at Nucor said that plant managers and vice presidents needed to develop their own careers. The new, enlightened philosophy: Nucor will help them become leaders. An internal trainer/coach now travels to all Nucor plants, engaging colleagues in what is called "NU Performance" training. As jobs change, the training helps workers keep current. Tools include training in the tried and tested Be-Know-Do (BKD) model of leadership development, expectations clarification, and a "Dollars and Tons" Monopoly-style game exercise designed to teach the economics of the steel business in an entertaining way. New managers are trained to be like deacons in a church: to be like servants, to not issue edicts, to not waste time in meetings, to not create task forces, to listen, to be accountable, to be out on the floor, and to encourage all employees to ask them questions.

Implicitly embracing the concept of *competere* (seeking together), each plant has its own set of books, including a profit and loss statement. What better way to encourage enlightened competition among plants, than by comparing them with the ultimate financial metric? Teams watch the bonus amounts of sister plants, and try to identify out what factors account for good performance there. Nucor, taking full advantage of employee initiative and self-management, will pay for employees to fly out to inspect best practices at other plants, where they engage in serious competitive benchmarking.

All Nucor employees anonymously participate in a yearly Mercer survey, consisting of about fifty questions. Generally rating Nucor highly, employees usually give high marks for pay and bonuses, and lower marks for promotion (there isn't much room to move up in the organization). The final survey question is: "If you could change one thing at Nucor, what would it be?" This crucial question yields rich data every year, turning up situations requiring immediate investigation and action.

Nucor tends to have the fewest accidents when production throughput is high and the factories are really humming. The company enjoys a superb quality safety culture, driven in part by the fact that injuries slow production, which costs bonus money.

Nucor does not conduct performance appraisals—they are considered a costly waste of time. As one manager put it: "I'll know if you're doing a good job by what other people say about you." Appraisals can even be counterproductive—a history of good appraisals combined with lack of promotion breeds frustration. Corporate HR colleagues serve as valued consultants to the plants; ensuring, for example, that plant managers hire and fire for the right reasons. Local administrators run the day-to-day human resource function at each plant.

Nucor internally posts all jobs from the supervisorial level and up. Each plant manager hires his or her respective department managers with assistance from headquarters, using a homegrown, validated psychological template that is highly predictive of leadership success. Nucor needs leaders that listen, are not overly judgmental or hot-tempered, think things through, and are willing to admit mistakes. They are trained to say "yes" to workers whenever they can, since they will need to say "no" frequently. Nucor strives to have a few crystal clear policies and very little documentation (although world markets are driving the need for more documentation, through initiatives like ISO 9000). Are employees free to speak up? At one facility, the workforce drafted and adopted it own hardhat policy—an example of self-management in action.

Another force binding employees to Nucor is the benefit package. One big hit: Nucor's employee scholarship program. The average education of Nucor employees is thirteen years. Nucor pays $3,000 per year for each college-age child of an employee, up to four years in college. The company recently had

790 children participating.[5] Nucor considers the foundation-run program its contribution to the future of America.

Other than its scholarship program, the standard benefits program is quite basic (think Chevrolet rather than Mercedes Benz). Nucor offers eight holidays, two weeks vacation (three after ten years), and a decent catastrophic PPO medical plan with no frills. Nucor shares its profits by investing 10% of the company's pre-tax earnings in an employee trust, with all employees below the VP level receiving a slice (based on the amount of their W-2 earnings as a percentage of all W-2s). The average payout in the last year (our interview took place in 2006) was $17,000 per employee (and it can be much less, especially when earnings fall). Employees participating in the Nucor 401(k) plan can receive an employer match of between 5% and 25% employer match based on their individual contribution level.

While not totally flat, Nucor does strive to obliterate the class distinctions that infect other companies—for example, putting the names of all 7,000 employees in its annual report, and communicating that leadership authority comes from people accepting you as a natural leader, not from title or position.[6]

Nucor exhibits several characteristics of self-management. It has a powerful unofficial justice system that massively leverages the leadership capabilities of its people, enabling them to be consultants, mentors and servants. It also has a strong performance culture driven by simple yet elegant feedback systems. The performance metrics (especially Quality Tons of Steel Per Week) fulfill the dual roles of driving throughput while reinforcing the justice system for employee accountability. Nucor has shown itself to be an excellent laboratory for organizational innovation.

⟨∽⟩

5   Jim Collins relates the story of the Nucor employee with nine children, who cried upon learning that the company would pay for four years of schooling for each of them. Collins, Jim *Good to Great.* Harper Business, 2001. 137.

6   Collins, Jim *Good to Great.* Harper Business, 2001. 138.

Delancey Street Foundation

In the world of life-changing organizations, the Delancey Street Foundation has few equals. Dr. Mimi Silbert's vision for a residential program to help people build lives with integrity and purpose, begun in 1971 in San Francisco, has spread to five additional locations around the United States. It has helped thousands of former drug users, convicts and destitute people restore their lives through effective and accountable self-management. Delancey Street's ability to run six facilities without staffing or funding is a testament to its amazing effectiveness—it never solicits funds or pursues donor development, because its own residents are the primary source of improvement. It is where people go when they have nowhere else to go. Where else can one find former gang enemies living side by side in perfect harmony?

A colleague and I toured the San Francisco headquarters facility by the bay on a bright spring day. Carol Kizziah, a project manager and consultant for Delancey Street since the 1970's (and intimately familiar with all aspects of the organization), greeted us warmly and directed us to an on-campus theater for an orientation and tour. Carol had been instrumental in coordinating with many key Delancey Street partnerships and projects over the years, and we looked forward to learning more from her after our tour.

Entering the theater, we were joined by a criminal justice class from a local law school, also there to learn about Delancey's recipe for success. Our tour guides were a man and woman who introduced themselves as having entered Delancey Street after hitting bottom. It was clear from their professional bearing that their past lives bore no resemblance to the present. They powerfully and movingly described their own personal journeys to Delancey Street, before escorting the group on an excellent tour.

Most residents stay at the facility for four years (the minimum stay is two years). Individuals come to Delancey Street as substance abusers or ex-convicts (or homeless), lacking in skills, and often functionally illiterate. In San Francisco, there are about 400 residents at any given time. To remain at Delancey

Street, they must avoid substance use and criminal behavior while obtaining a GED and at least three marketable skills. Delancey Street augments the hard skills with the training in values and social skills to enable future personal and professional effectiveness.

To become a resident of Delancey Street, a person must volunteer. And it is not necessarily easy to gain admission: current residents conduct tough admission interviews, and they don't allow prevarication. Like most people, residents only want to live in a community with people they can reasonably trust. Delancey Street wants to create a very safe environment where people can practice being adults who are capable of change. Criminal courts may grant individuals the opportunity to apply to live at Delancey Street, if appropriate for the situation (certain classes of crime, like arson, will render a prospective resident unsuitable). Judges, aware of Delancey Street's success over the last four decades, would rather have a convict turn his or her life around than remain stuck in the revolving door of the justice system.

Interestingly, although Delancey Street prefaces each guest tour with a brief orientation, there is no formal orientation for new residents. Delancey relies on a strong oral tradition to acculturate new residents quickly. A core principle of Delancey Street is "each-one-teach-one"—the idea that each new resident is required to help the next new resident become oriented to the values and expectations of the facility. This simple yet highly effective mentoring rule insures that all residents not only receive the core Delancey Street values, but that new residents reinforce the values by teaching them to others. The values include hard work, accountability and respect. One quickly-absorbed core value is a zero-tolerance policy toward acts or threats of violence. Either will trigger immediate eviction. Unsurprisingly, people tend to behave themselves once admitted.

Our tour concluded, we sat down with Carol and learned more about education and work, accountability and the culture of transformation.

Education and Work

Delancey Street uses an education-based model. It views education as critical for residents in building a self-respecting, self-managing adult identity. Delancey Street refers to itself as a total learning center[7], where education isn't something that just happens in a classroom, but is inculcated through academics, work, mentoring, and everyday life.

At Delancey Street, education embraces all skills needed for a successful adult life, including social and interpersonal skills. Delancey Street requires each resident to teach others throughout their experience there (each-one-teach-one). This one-to-one mentoring takes place wherever and whenever necessary— at school, at work, or at social functions.

In addition to entering one of several vocational training schools, each resident is required to obtain a GED. The system operates on a semester basis with "study abroad" opportunities: a resident who entered the program in San Francisco, for example, may take the Delancey Street bus to the program in New York for a semester. A major key is making people feel successful, so they will create success by breaking old, bad habits and replacing them with new, effective ones. Delancey Street wants people to focus on their strengths, not their weaknesses.

Delancey Street asks people to work hard. It has created twelve businesses using a social entrepreneurship model—teaching business skills to solve social problems. San Francisco has a café and bookstore, a restaurant, a moving business, and several others. Delancey assigns each resident to a business and provides a mentor. Residents start at the bottom and work their way up, building a strong work ethic in the process—which local employers have learned to appreciate.

Delancey Street believes in placing residents in jobs outside their comfort zone. For example, a former chef may be assigned to work in landscaping instead of the restaurant, thereby teaching humility. While Delancey Street is willing to try new entrepreneurial ventures, it accepts that not all of them will pan out. New ventures should be very labor intensive and extremely simple to

7   http://www.delanceystreetfoundation.org/wwb.php

run. Residents can earn greater decision rights and authority based on job performance and energy level—encouraging hard work and integrity.

As Delancey Street puts it:

Economic development and **entrepreneurial boldness** are central to our model's financial self-sufficiency and to teaching residents self-reliance and life skills.[8]

Accountability

Delancey Street has a powerful culture of accountability. It relies on its residents to acculturate newcomers quickly and effectively.

Residents are expected to immediately call out their fellow residents on behavior detrimental to the facility, its residents or the culture. If a resident sees someone doing something wrong—and ignores it—he or she is as guilty as the rule breaker. Delancey Street residents don't shy away from confrontation, they embrace it. Residents regard confrontation as the opposite of snitching—it is a willingness to help the other person out of care and concern.

While direct communication is usually desirable, its appropriateness may depend on the circumstances. Very serious issues are taken to a council of residents for resolution.

While residents are free to leave Delancey Street, they are never alone there—someone is always watching out for them. Delancey Street provides a highly structured environment where people learn how to develop adult skills, reinforced by small groups and the culture itself. At Delancey Street, peer pressure is the strongest force for growth and change.

Culture

The culture at Delancey Street feels like a very large family—because that's exactly what it is. There is no staff of experts to "fix" people according to a therapeutic model. Delancey Street embraces an "AS-IF" philosophy—it encourages residents to behave AS IF they are decent people of integrity from day one,

---

8   http://www.delanceystreetfoundation.org/wwb.php

regardless of their past or present circumstances. Over time, residents come to understand that they *are* hard working, decent people of integrity—because that's what they have learned to become.

Delancey Street pays close attention to the little things—encouraging excellence and confronting mistakes. Delancey people acknowledge little wins, because they add up over time and are easier to achieve than big wins. Personal growth is an incremental, day-by-day process.

Each resident is assigned to a "tribe", or peer group within the facility. Each resident meets with his or her tribe to have a frequent, honest facilitated discussion about areas for improvement. Once residents get past the initial shock of unvarnished peer feedback, the sessions provide a powerful guide to individual improvement.

Delancey Street encourages frequent, effective communication. And it keeps people busy virtually all the time. When residents aren't working or being tutored for the GED, they are attending peer groups, parenting workshops, seminars, dances or debates—frequently at lunchtime. Delancey Street has a powerful culture of continuous, engaging action. And it works—creating thousands of self-reliant, self-managing people of integrity. Isn't that what all businesses need?

Morning Star

Introduction

California entrepreneur Chris Rufer started Morning Star[9] as a trucking company in 1970, beginning with one truck. While driving his truck in the summer to put himself through college, he began to notice how the factories where he delivered his loads were often inefficient and poorly run.

Equipped with an MBA, he crafted a business plan for a tomato processing plant that would produce industrial tomato paste in efficient bulk containers for worldwide distribution. His formula for success would be to know his customers and suppliers well, and be the low-cost producer. He spent endless hours identifying the right combinations of process equipment to achieve maximum throughput and efficiency. Finally, Chris brought together a group of grower-partners and began construction of his first successful food processing plant, Ingomar Packing Company, in 1982.

Following Ingomar's success, Chris formed The Morning Star Packing Company to process tomatoes near the small town of Los Banos, California. In the spring of 1990, a tiny farmhouse on the outskirts of town became a beehive of round-the-clock activity. Cars and pickups parked all over the yard, shaded by oak trees. The kitchen became a conference room, where an endless parade of job applicants, bankers, regulators, vendors, and contractors met together in nonstop organizational meetings. Desk lamps burned late into the night; sleep was in short supply.

Chris and his team focused with intensity on getting the new factory up and running. Tomato plants were already in the ground, growing. A successful startup would declare an entirely new level of industry competition. Most of Morning Star's new employees had left secure jobs to join the team. If the venture failed, there would be short-term personal disruption, but all could find new jobs. For Chris, however, everything was at risk.

---

9   After the final sentence in Thoreau's *Walden Pond*: The sun is but a morning star.

Stakeholder obligations and personal guarantees created high stakes–folding one's cards was not an option.

The first loads of tomatoes arrived at Morning Star's first new state-of-the-art facility in mid-July of 1990 and kicked off a successful season, producing over ninety million pounds of bulk tomato paste for the world market.

The Morning Star Packing Company built its second advanced facility in Williams, California, in 1995. This facility replaced its original namesake as the largest tomato processing factory in the world. Chris later purchased an existing vacant (and somewhat dilapidated) factory near Los Banos, gave it a thorough renovation, and commissioned Liberty Packing Company in 2002, dedicated to the production of bulk tomato paste, diced tomatoes, and canned products. He also created custom harvesting operations to optimize the supply chain with trucking and manufacturing.

Morning Star has never pursued growth for the sake of growth; the focus has always been on technical innovation combined with very good execution. Morning Star has grown, however, in response to world market demand for low-cost, high-quality bulk tomato products. At home and around the world, people just seem to enjoy the flavor of tomatoes in their food. As of this writing, the three California Morning Star processing facilities are the largest individual plants in the industry. Together, they comprise the largest tomato processing company in the world.

While Morning Star owes much of its success to its low-cost strategy, culture of innovation and process execution, a good measure of its success is also attributable to a unique organizational philosophy: self-management.

Organizational Philosophy

Morning Star implemented its self-management philosophy of in 1990, with the construction of its first factory.

The primary characteristic of this philosophy is flatness. The organization is designed to be as flat as a floor, with absolutely no hierarchy. There are no directive human bosses; the only boss is the company Mission statement. The philosophy is one of total self-management. Morning Star employees refer to themselves as colleagues, and consider themselves professionals in their respective roles.

Command authority doesn't exist in the company, even on the part of the owner (barring unusual circumstances with legal ramifications). Consequently, there is no unilateral authority to fire. Acquiring or concluding the services of other colleagues must be accomplished according to a clear set of established principles incorporating due process.

No one in the organization has a title, which sometimes creates confusion for those outside the organization, but serves to reinforce Morning Star's flatness within the organization (the back of every title-free Morning Star business card reads *Excellence Through Commitment*).

While lacking formal structure, there are resources available to help colleagues synchronize their activities with others. Each colleague executes a Colleague Letter of Understanding (also known as a CLOU). The CLOU is an accountability agreement between colleagues declaring each individual's personal commercial mission, business process responsibilities, scope of decision authority, and performance measures.

Morning Star's success takes place in a complex and demanding business environment. As an organization, Morning Star must grapple with subjects like plant genetics, microbiology, food chemistry, thermodynamics, and meteorology. Individually, Morning Star colleagues continuously navigate the business risks and opportunities impacted by these disciplines. The Colleague Letter of Understanding is a key navigational device, answering the question: where should I focus my efforts?

The Morning Star culture is very conducive to self-managing, mature individuals. It can be a challenging environment for those who need to be told what to do, or who are themselves directive toward others. In the utter absence of position power, leadership responsibility must be earned.

There is as much need for leadership in a self-managed organization as in a hierarchical one, it's just that self-managed leadership is dynamic rather than static—it depends on the issue and the individuals. Leadership in such an ecosystem can rotate and evolve naturally, depending on the circumstances. No particular leadership style is required, and many leadership styles can work well.

Ultimately, the foundation of shared bedrock values creates an environment where successful colleagues can mentor others and help them navigate successfully.

• Company Mission
The Mission of The Morning Star Company is simple:

Our Mission is to produce tomato products that consistently achieve the product and service expectations of our customers in a cost effective, environmentally responsible manner. We will provide bulk-packaged products to food processors and customer-branded, finished products to the food service and retail trade.[10]

The first sentence is a simple declaration of purpose. The second sentence describes the two business domains that Morning Star supplies.

Morning Star generally doesn't strive to exceed customer expectations. Tomato products are commodities, and customers will usually not pay extra for exceeded expectations. According to Chris Rufer, business is a dynamic adventure of balancing the needs of customers, suppliers, employees, and society at large, and using resources appropriately and efficiently. That philosophy is the essence of the Morning Star Mission.

• Company Vision
The company vision of Olympic Gold Medal Performance[11] contains several elements.

The first element is one of total responsibility. While each Morning Star colleague is identified with specific business processes, no one is allowed to ignore a known issue with the excuse that 'it's not my problem.' All colleagues have an affirmative

---

10　See Appendix for an expanded version.

11　See Appendix.

obligation to report any issue that comes into their field of vision to other pertinent colleagues.

The second element is clarity of vision. This is primarily accomplished through the creation of a personal commercial mission for each colleague, congruent with the overall company Mission.

The third element is the creative advancement of technology. This element recognizes that innovation is the only source of long-term competitive advantage. Patents expire, trade secrets disappear. An entire organization dedicated to innovation and learning cannot be easily duplicated.

The last element of values is foundational to the Morning Star philosophy. These values include integrity (which actually improves economic business value for individuals and companies by lowering transaction costs), openness, and physically attractive facilities.

• Colleague Principles

Relationships at Morning Star are governed by a set of Colleague Principles[12]. These Principles have several key features.

The Principles (to which colleagues agree to adhere) require several commitments. First, colleagues agree to embrace the Mission.

Second, colleagues agree to commit to individual goals (specified in the Colleague Letter of Understanding) and teamwork (which requires, by definition, communication).

Third, colleagues agree to accept personal responsibility and take initiative.

Fourth, colleagues agree to tolerate non-work-related differences in the interest of teamwork.

There are several corollaries to this set of principles. One is the requirement of direct communication with colleagues. Since there are no supervisors to process complaints about individuals, each person must address issues directly with their colleagues. There is simply no other way to get things done. An ombudsman is available when someone seeks confidential advice regarding

12   See Appendix.

an issue. Ultimately, however, the burden of communication remains with the individual colleague.

Another corollary is that differences shall be resolved privately, if possible. The Principles describe a process for gaining agreement one-on-one, then bringing in a third party to mediate if the initial discussion fails to achieve resolution, and finally bringing the issue to a panel of peers as the final step in resolution.

A further corollary is that information shall be shared with colleagues, even if not requested. This places an affirmative obligation on each colleague to forward pertinent information to others that may be helpful to them in accomplishing their respective missions. There is no excuse for hoarding or hiding information. Prodigious information sharing is a key Morning Star strength, and contributes greatly to organizational agility. Information permeates the entire enterprise—and there are no structural barriers to sharing information anywhere in the company.

The requirement of following these principles demands selection process rigor. The selection process generally includes multiple interviews and a battery of diagnostics. New hires have come from the U.S. Navy, the semiconductor industry, and many other diverse backgrounds. Morning Star strives to place "A" players in every position. The overall Vision is that of Olympic Gold Medal Performance.

Every Morning Star colleague is considered a professional. Each Morning Star electrician and mechanic, for example, is personally responsible for the operation and maintenance of equipment valued in the millions. Electricians and mechanics conduct payback analyses on capital project proposals. They deal personally with vendors, seasonal colleagues, and sometimes customers. In addition, they personally perform the operational and maintenance work needed to run each factory. Each full-time production colleague accepts total stewardship for his or her slice of the factory.

For an individual electro-mechanic's agreed orbit of responsibility, documented in the CLOU, accountability for performance lies with no one else.

Power of Self-Management

The power of self-management can be seen in two areas.

First, Morning Star is a principle-driven enterprise. Its two core principles are: 1) individuals should honor their commitments to others, and 2) individuals should not exercise the use of force against other people (or the property of other people). Human beings tend to experience greater harmony and prosperity in life when they acknowledge and act in accordance with these simple, yet profound principles.

Colleagues take commitments seriously at Morning Star. Even ad hoc commitments undertaken between two colleagues passing in the hallway on a low or medium level business matter may be documented, and fulfillment expected. In the absence of command authority there is no other way to get things done with others. There may not be human bosses, but there may be many colleagues to whom one is fully accountable for various commitments.

The total absence of command authority (or force) means that people have no choice but to seek commitment from others through influence and persuasion, rather than outright direction. While this usually takes longer than issuing commands, it does ensure consultation with all stakeholders in a decision. It also ensures the sharing of information—and usually results in better decisions.

The lack of position power also presents a key test for aspiring leaders. In an environment devoid of command authority, respect and credibility must be earned. The question for a potential leader becomes: how effective is your leadership when no one is required to follow you?

Second, the organization enjoys a high degree of agility to deal with opportunities and threats, and strengths and weaknesses. Colleagues are able to use their freedom to continuously improve business processes, for example. No Morning Star process is off-limits to analysis, experimentation and improvement.

Self-Management Requirements

Effective self-management requires several ingredients.

First, self-managed freedom must be balanced with responsibility. Freedom without responsibility is unproductive. Responsibility without freedom is frustrating. Morning Star strives to achieve a harmonious balance between the two.

Second, colleagues must completely understand their tasks, goals and values. This primarily consists of having a deep understanding of the business processes for which they are partly or fully responsible. Short-term or long-term goals may be either business-related or personal.

Third, taking initiative is a major key to effective self-management. For self-management to work, colleagues must display initiative in all areas. This includes initiating the acquisition and termination of the services of fellow colleagues. In addition, colleagues are fully responsible for their own training. It is never an excuse at Morning Star to say that one was not trained to perform his or her job.

Finally, self-management requires integrity, a characteristic that actually improves business value. When suppliers, customers, and co-workers can count on a colleague's word, the cost of doing business actually decreases and business value increases–a key success factor.

Activity Feedback

Activity feedback is critical to success in a self-managed environment.

First, self-management requires performance measurement, since no one can manage him or herself without knowing how well they are performing in the first place. There are no supervisors or managers to provide evaluations.

Second, continuous process improvement requires measurement, since it is impossible to know if a process is improving or deteriorating without a mechanism in place to convey reality. Results that are declining or are not improving are often indicators of a business process that needs immediate attention.

Third, Morning Star measures performance against both perfection and reality. It's a good bet that the world's greatest golfer will never shoot an 18. But it's also reasonable to assume that if a golfer strives for an 18, he'll be more likely to improve than if he strives for, say, a 78. Morning Star identifies perfect results for each and every business process, creating a vision of perfect performance for each colleague. Morning Star also identifies more realistic and achievable goals for each process. The ultimate goal is to transform work into a game, and to make it an enjoyable voyage of discovery.

Self-Management: Desired Results

The first key benefit from self-management is the concept of "enlightened competition" (again, like Nucor, from the idea of *competere*, or "seeking together"). Self-management gives Morning Star colleagues the freedom to seek best practices from each other within a facility, from other Morning Star facilities, and externally. Annual inter-company functional area meetings provide a forum for these "compare and contrast" discussions.

A second desired result from self-management is the effectiveness, efficiency and ultimate profitability of the enterprise, created by the lofty performance of engaged and enthusiastic colleagues.

Colleague Letter of Understanding (CLOU)

One of the key self-management tools available to Morning Star colleagues is the Colleague Letter of Understanding (CLOU).

The CLOU (essentially, a performance contract between colleagues) accomplishes several things.

First, it defines overall responsibilities of colleagues in terms of the Vision, Mission and Principles.

Second, it identifies the specific responsibilities and commitments for each colleague.

Third, the CLOU documents various colleague representations, including each colleague's declaration of commercial competence to perform their mission.

The parties to a particular colleague's CLOU are generally the internal customers and suppliers who engage in business process hand-offs with the colleague. A typical Morning Star colleague will likely have about six or seven CLOU signatories.

These are the people to whom a Morning Star colleague owes the most in terms of time and attention.

- **Overall CLOU Responsibilities**

First, in addition to emphasizing the Vision, Mission and Principles, the CLOU requires each colleague to be responsible for all business processes reasonably within their scope of awareness. Colleagues agree to take the initiative to deal with issues within their control, as well as issues that come into their field of vision, regardless of whether the colleague is normally responsible for those issues.

Morning Star has undertaken to document its business processes and decisions, identifying event triggers, information requirements, inputs and outputs. It is incumbent on each colleague to master the processes within his or her control.

Second, colleagues agree to undertake a specific level of effort (expressed in terms of expected hours per week).

Finally, colleagues are expected to align their personal business process activities with the Vision and Mission of the enterprise

- **Specific CLOU Responsibilities**

The CLOU identifies specific colleague responsibilities in the form of a matrix that defines each colleague's personal commercial mission (again, aligned with the overall company Mission). For example, the mission of a front-end mechanic might be: "To create a vast and beautiful tropical tomato juice bowl for the evaporation process." Personal commercial missions are often simple, mnemonic and to the point.

The specific commitments matrix outlines the specific business processes for which the colleague is responsible, the decision authority affixed to each process for that colleague (Decide, Recommend, or Act or some combination thereof), the specific performance measures (called Steppingstones) that pertain to each process, and the reporting intervals for each metric.

There is little or no discussion of empowerment at Morning Star, because colleagues have all the power they need to get the job done from the first day of work. There are no inherent barriers for anyone seeking any resource necessary to accomplish the Mission. Everyone is as free as everyone else at Morning Star to communicate, initiate action, innovate and execute.

- **General CLOU Obligations**

The CLOU also contains several general obligations for each colleague. These include certain commitments to continuing education and training, notification of observed risk situations, commitment to collaboration, and appropriate handling of proprietary information.

Steppingstones (Key Performance Indicators)

Each business process needs to be monitored for performance. Morning Star refers to its performance measures as "Steppingstones", considered steppingstones to perfect performance (even if one never quite arrives there). Colleagues identify Steppingstones pertinent to their individual business processes. Each process may have one or more Steppingstones attached to it. Steppingstones may be common to several colleagues (who may be responsible for the same process), or they may be unique to an individual. The frequency of publication is appropriate to the specific process (some financial measures are quarterly, many production measures are hourly).

Each Morning Star factory historically measures a few hundred Steppingstones covering all facets of production, administration, distribution, raw materials acquisition, quality, marketing and sales. The ultimate Steppingstone is, of course, return on assets. Without a positive return on assets over time, there wouldn't be a company in the first place.

Steppingstones data, to the degree possible, are subject to inquiry by any colleague at any time. Usually consisting of time-series data, Morning Star strives to update and display Steppingstones data in a way that facilitates enlightened competition between colleagues at different factories, and encourages experimentation, information sharing and the implementation of best business practices.

Trying to self-manage without receiving appropriate performance feedback would be like trying to fly a 747 without a functional navigation system. People need to know where they are relative to where they want to go. The company provides resources to help people navigate, make decisions, communicate and act—but ultimately, people have to manage themselves and their relationships. Managing oneself and one's work relationships around innovation and execution represents the essential core of self-management.

As business process authority Roger T. Burlton wrote in his book *Business Process Management: Profiting from Process*, "Morning Star is the best example I've seen of a mature process-managed company. Nowhere else have I witnessed or even heard of a company that's so driven to manage its relationships in such a natural way—totally process-empowered and a great place to work."[13]

---

13   Burlton, Roger T. *Business Process Management: Profiting from Process.* Sams Publishing, 2001. 105.

Appendix

ᘯ

The Morning Star Company Mission, Vision and Colleague Principles

Our Mission

Our Mission is to produce tomato products that consistently achieve the product and service expectations of our customers in a cost effective, environmentally responsible manner. We will provide bulk-packaged products to food processors and customer-branded, finished products to the food service and retail trade.

We will use the most appropriate tomato products manufacturing technologies available, properly assembled in new factories to take advantage of their individual strengths and economies. We will creatively match human talent and technologies to continuously achieve customer expectations for great product quality and to lower costs of operations (conserve resources). We will focus and build our talents for around-the-clock, people coordinating operations utilizing material conveying and pumping, structural, motor, electrical, automation, steam generation, heat transfer, aseptic, fluids and food formulating and preservation technologies.

Our Vision

To be an Olympic Gold Medal performer in the tomato products industry. To develop and implement superior systems of organizing individuals' talents and efforts to achieve demonstrably superior productivity and personal happiness. To develop and implement superior technology and production systems which significantly and demonstrably increase the effective use of resources that match customers' requirements. To provide opportunity for more harmonious and prosperous lives, bringing happiness to ourselves and the people we serve.

Colleague Self-Management

For Morning Star colleagues to be Self-Managing Professionals, initiating communications and the coordination of their activities with fellow colleagues, customers, suppliers and fellow industry participants, absent directives from others. For colleagues to find joy and excitement utilizing their unique talents and to weave those talents into activities which complement and strengthen fellow colleagues' activities. For colleagues to take personal responsibility and hold themselves accountable for achieving our Mission and shaping the Tomato and Fruit Game.

Clarity of Vision

For Morning Star colleagues to develop a clear vision of perfect results and how their personal commercial mission relates to achieving our customers' tomato and fruit product requirements. To achieve demonstrably superior efficiency in the use of environmental resources to create our products. To measure and present our performance in the context of perfect results and to use this vision to drive our decision making and actions.

Creative Advancement of Technology

For Morning Star colleagues to develop significant, creative technological advances in tomato and fruit products production methods. Only when we achieve this, will we dedicate additional significant resources to expand production or produce different products.

Values

To work with fellow colleagues, customers, suppliers and industry participants within a framework of solid integrity and openness in pursuit of voluntary and mutually beneficial transactions and relationships. To maintain our facilities in a clean and orderly condition with a pleasant appearance.

Colleague Principles

In order to encourage, achieve and maintain an atmosphere of high integrity, trust, competence and harmony among all colleagues, customers and suppliers, each Morning Star Colleague commits to the following:

1. Mission. Our Mission is to produce tomato products that consistently achieve the product and service expectations of our customers in a cost effective, environmentally responsible manner. We will provide bulk-packaged products to food processors and customer-branded, finished products to the food service and retail trade.

2. Individual Goals and Teamwork. We hereby agree to commit ourselves to the pursuit of perfection with regard to our integrity, competence and individual responsibility. In recognition of each Colleague's personal goal of achieving happiness, each of us commits to pursue teamwork because Together Everyone Accomplishes More.

3. Personal Responsibility and Initiative. We agree to take full responsibility for our actions as well as those of fellow Colleagues and our overall Mission. We are personally responsible for our training, time commitments, performance and participating in and contributing toward achieving the Mission and practicing the Principles. We commit to manage ourselves, to personally take the initiative to coordinate our responsibilities and activities with other Colleagues, to develop opportunities for improvement and for <u>making things happen</u>.

4. Tolerance. It is understood that individuals differ in many ways–their values, tastes, moods and methods to achieve goals. It is agreed that these types of differences between individual Colleagues will be respected and tolerated.

5. Direct Communication and Gaining Agreement. Differences between human beings are a natural and necessary aspect of life, especially in the pursuit of excellence. Differences may vary from how to answer the phone, to what type of oil to use in a gearbox, to what equipment to

purchase to improve operations, to whether one is following our Principles or advancing our Mission, to how a person combs their hair. To gain agreement and move forward, we agree to utilize the following the process:

- When one Colleague perceives a difference with another, we agree to privately discuss the matter with the other Colleague as soon as practical and attempt to resolve any differences to our mutual satisfaction. As a general rule, we will not discuss such matters with other Colleagues. However, if a Colleague feels uneasy directly discussing a matter regarding another Colleague, then they should go to another Colleague to discuss alternatives for solving the issue, keeping in mind that confidence should be maintained with their chosen ombudsman.

- If either of the Colleagues do not feel the matter has been resolved to their satisfaction, then both of them agree to discuss the matter, together, with one other Colleague as soon as practical and attempt to resolve any differences to our mutual satisfaction with the help of the third Colleague.

- If either of the Colleagues still do not feel the matter has been resolved to their satisfaction, then both of them agree to discuss the matter with a contingent of approximately three (3) to ten (10) Colleagues appropriate for the particular matter.

- If either of the Colleagues still do not feel the matter has been resolved to their satisfaction, then both of them agree to discuss the matter with the designated Colleagues and the President of Morning Star.

- In attempting to resolve differences, the following shall be given careful consideration: A) our Mission and any specific objective; B) the relevant facts, assumptions and values; and C) the method used to determine the proper direction. Other courses of action, upon mutual agreement among the affected Colleagues are encouraged, however, either party has the option of requiring the above steps to be taken at their request.

- When there is a determination on a course of action for the facility Colleagues, or specific Colleagues, it is incumbent on each Colleague to follow that course of action. If new, material information becomes available which could change the chosen course of action regarding any particular matter, then it should be presented for consideration and a new determination. Until a new course of action is determined, each Colleague agrees to follow the chosen course of action and work energetically toward achieving the Mission in the manner decided.

6. Caring and Sharing. To the degree Colleagues care about themselves, their friends and relatives, fellow Colleagues, suppliers, customers, the environment, the Mission, Principles and facilities, etc., each of us will come closer to achieving our personal goals. In caring for others, each Colleague commits to (1) sharing relevant information with others, (2) taking the initiative to forward information that they believe may be helpful to other's activities, even if it is not asked for, and (3) responding to respectful inquiries made of them by other Colleagues in a respectful and responsive manner.

7. Doing What is Right. Living, speaking and endeavoring to find the truth.

About The Morning Star Self-Management Institute

www.self-managementinstitute.org

Our Mission

Our Mission is to develop superior principles and systems of organizing people, and to promulgate those principles and systems in the minds of our client colleagues.

Our Vision

We envision a flourishing community of self-managed enterprises, operating wholly pursuant to the principles–and effectively utilizing the tools–developed and perpetuated by our Institute.

We believe that the principles of Self-Management, when wholly understood, yield a superior organizational structure and happier, more efficient, colleagues. Together, the individual freedom and authority resulting from a truly Self-Managed enterprise yield an environment that mimics closely the principles, and progressive human benefits, of a free-market economy.

13563915R00090

Made in the USA
Lexington, KY
07 February 2012